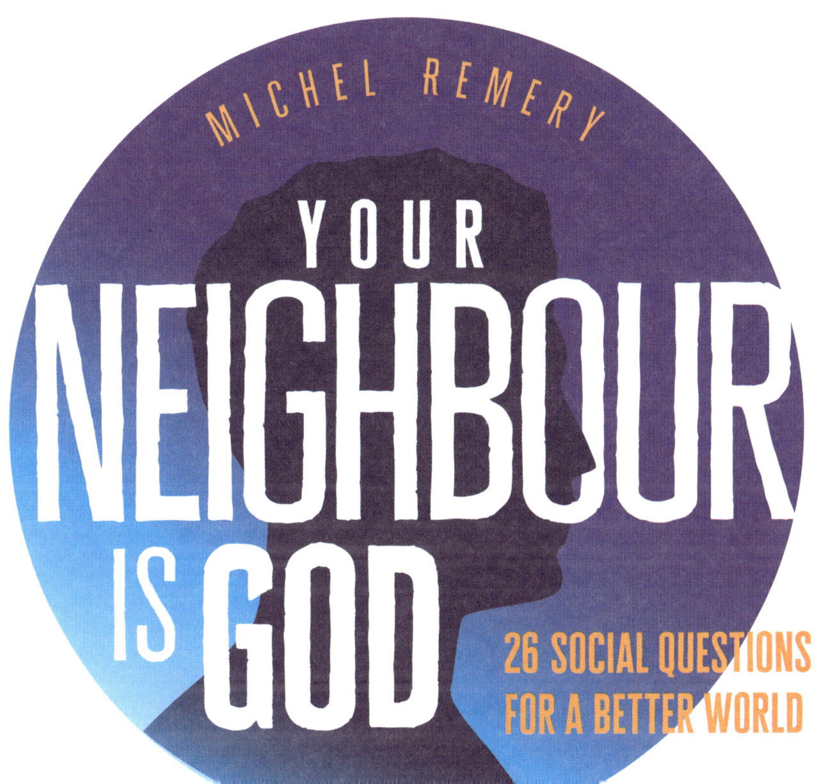

POWERED BY

APPEAL FOR DONATIONS

If you can and wish to contribute financially to our initiatives we would be very grateful. You can transfer your donation via the website www.tweetingwithgod.com/donate or directly to the following bank account:

Bank: ING Bank
Account holder: JP2 Stichting Leiden
Mention: "Tweeting with GOD"
IBAN: NL31 INGB 0005717224
BIC/SWIFT: INGBNL2A

Address of the bank:
ING Bank NV Foreign Operations
P.O. Box 1800
NL-1000 BV Amsterdam
The Netherlands

The JP2 Foundation, based in Leiden, The Netherlands, was set up to cover the financial and contractual aspects of our projects. For its income, this non-profit organisation depends entirely on the help of sponsors. All donations are used for funding our projects only. If you send us your address, you will receive a confirmation of your donation.

We thank you in advance for your generosity!

www.tweetingwithgod.com/donate

YOUR NEIGHBOUR IS GOD

26 SOCIAL QUESTIONS FOR A BETTER WORLD

www.yourneighbourisgod.com

Developed by the makers of ***Tweeting with GOD, Online with Saints,*** and ***How to grow in faith***

www.tweetingwithgod.com | www.onlinewithsaints.com | www.howtogrowinfaith.com

Nihil obstat: Rev Gerard Diamond MA (Oxon), LSS, D.Theol, diocesan censor
Imprimatur: Rev Mgr Joseph Caddy AM Lic.Soc.Sci. VG, vicar general
Archdiocese of Melbourne, 27 February 2021

Graphic design & cover by Gustavo Huguenin

Photo Credits: Shutterstock, Unsplash.com.

Scripture quotations have been taken from the New Revised Standard Version, Anglicised Catholic Edition, © 1989 by the Division of Christian Education of the National Council of the Churches of Christ in the United States of America, or are translated by the author.

Quotations from the popes and the official documents of the Catholic Church are from the Vatican website www.vatican.va. All rights reserved.

Excerpts from the Catechism of the Catholic Church, Second Edition, © 2000 by Libreria Editrice Vaticana-United States Conference of Catholic Bishops, Washington, D.C, or www.vatican.va. All rights reserved.

Other than for the purposes and subject to the conditions prescribed under the Copyright Act, no part of this publication may be reproduced, stored in a retrieval system, or transmitted in any form or by any means, electronic, mechanical, photocopying, recording or otherwise, without the prior permission of the publisher.

© 2020 Michel Remery & JP2 Stichting, Leiden. All rights reserved.

Published 2021 by Freedom Publishing books, Melbourne. All rights reserved.

Printed in Australia by Brougham Press | ISBN 9781922589040

www.yourneighbourisgod.com

TABLE OF CONTENTS

POVERTY & SOLIDARITY

ENVIRONMENT & ANIMAL RIGHTS

JUSTICE & PEACE

ECONOMY & WORK

POLITICS & STATE

TECHNOLOGY & FAITH SHARING

APPENDICES

PREFACE

So what if God lived next door to you? What would you do? What would you not do? You will probably not fall on your knees for the woman or man next door to adore them as a deity… But sometimes you do indeed have to fall on your knees to help another human being in need. Jesus said that whatever you do for someone who is hungry, thirsty, homeless, naked, sick, or imprisoned, you do to him! *(Mt 25:35-36).*

I must admit that when my neighbour is a likeable old lady, it is easy to do something extra for her. I might even recognise something of God in her. But I find this more difficult when a dirty and smelly homeless person yells at me because they consider my donation too small. God needs me to be his hands and feet – and his mouth too. While I can only do so much, I *can* help my neighbour! By doing so my faith in God becomes real and tangible.

Celebrate

When the occasion presents itself, I love sailing, a meal with friends, or very dark chocolate. But can I really enjoy such treats when somewhere else my brothers and sisters are suffering? Is life not about more serious things? Well, Jesus' first miracle was to change water into good wine *(Jn 2:1-11).* That wine served no other purpose than to celebrate with joy in an imperfect world. We too should celebrate at times, and always be joyful. Jesus wants our joy to be complete *(Jn 15:11).* Therefore, the next day he continued to preach the Gospel to the poor and marginalised.

While it is great to enjoy an occasional material treat and praise God for it, the Bible tells me of the rich fool who filled his barns with grain and goods, only to die when he had accumulated all this wealth *(Lk 12:15-21).* Instead of worrying about what I will eat or wear, I should only strive for God's Kingdom *(Lk 12:22-31).* In everything I do, I should strive to make the world a better place!

Hope

Everything around us will change one day. The only certainty is God's promise of eternal life in his presence in heaven. That promise of supernatural life is precisely what makes it worth the struggle (not just the food or drink)! When I share my bread with people around me, it would be very unfair not to tell them of that hopeful promise too!

Our life now is somewhat like a camping trip. We are happy to accept some discomfort when travelling, knowing that in a few days or weeks we will be home again with everything we (think we) need. If heaven is our home, life on earth is but a camping holiday with some uncomfortable elements. Knowing what awaits us in heaven hopefully makes it easier to share what I have with my neighbour. Thus I can contribute to a better world.

Develop

God has given us a brain to develop our situation in life. And indeed we have: from the first caves and animal skins to protect our vulnerable bodies, we have moved on to well-designed houses and clothing, with forms that please both minds and senses. But not everyone has access to these. Our creative brain comes with a responsibility to care and to share.

While some of our inventions are good and advance the well-being of humankind, others harm people or God's creation. This is true for my personal life too. Every time when I prepare for my confession, I realise once more that I have acted against love for God and my neighbour, and that I have hurt them by my sins.

Planting trees

It is our mission to make this imperfect life on earth as bearable as possible for all. Like the popes, I can contribute by planting trees. Trees that will provide oxygen and feed people with their fruits long after my death. I can also plant spiritual trees of hope, by spreading the great message of God's love and his promise of our final destiny with him. When others pass this message on, also these spiritual trees continue to bear fruit long after my death.

The following pages show that life on earth is about caring for your neighbour and God's creation in the broadest sense. You will hopefully know from experience that sharing makes you happy. Who cares that it is always you who bring that perfect bottle of wine or chocolate bar? It is only truly perfect when enjoyed in good company! Similarly, our life only nears its perfection when experienced together with our creator, God. He waits ardently for us in our heavenly home. He is also here with us, especially in your neighbour, the small, poor, and needy – hoping and trusting that we will come to meet him.

Father Michel Remery

/FatherMichelRemery

@FrMichelRemery

ABOUT THIS BOOK

The origin of this book lies in questions that you will probably be asking yourself. Each of the questions has been asked by young and not so young people from around the world. This also explains the choice of topics. The answers give you a great overview of what the Church has to say about these themes.

Look at Jesus

You will see that to many questions we cannot give a simple yes/no answer as is the case with certain questions in ***Tweeting with GOD*** *(see below)*. Things are more fluid here. Life cannot be caught in a binary system of yes/no. To find a comprehensive answer we need to look at Jesus and see how he deals with people and situations. He does so always with love, always with care, and always with justice. He invites you to do the same. Thinking about the many questions raised here will help you further develop your view on the world.

Conscience

You have been created by God in his image and likeness *(Gen 1:26)*, and traces of him can be recognised in you - even if you do not acknowledge God. He gave you your conscience, which helps you to remain very close to who you really are and how God intends you to be. Consequently, your conscience is a safe guide in life, as long as you listen to it honestly and selflessly. To do this properly, you need to 'inform' your conscience: the more you learn about God and his choices, the better you will be able to interpret your conscience. The Holy Spirit wants to help you with his inspiration. You can always pray and ask for his help.

Principles

A great tool to help inform your conscience are the principles of the social teaching of the Church *(see Basics)*. These principles, based on Jesus' teaching of justice and love in the Bible, are applicable always and everywhere. When we look at individual questions, we will refer over and again to these principles *(see Basics)*. Furthermore, also daily prayer, spiritual accompaniment, and asking advice from wise Christians are great ways to inform your conscience further.

Proclaim

All the principles of the social teaching are based on the Gospel, which is intended to be announced to everyone *(Mt 28:19-20)*. The ultimate aim of this book is to help you live your life as a Christian. To do so means sharing the message of the Gospel with others around you. Proclaiming the good news of a life with Jesus is not done first of all from a pedestal on the marketplace or in a church, but through your way of life and gentle explanation 'of the hope that is in you' *(1 Pt 3:15)*. With Jesus life is never totally dark, there is always a perspective. There is always hope. This hopeful message can change the world.

THE WORKS OF MERCY

The Church recognises seven Corporal and seven Spiritual Works of Mercy *(see #TwGOD 4.7)*. These are based on the teachings and example of Jesus, who calls us to take care of both the body and the soul of our fellow human beings *(Mt 25:35-37 & 28:19-20)*.

Corporal Works of Mercy

1. Feed the hungry
2. Give drink to the thirsty
3. Clothe the naked
4. Shelter the homeless
5. Visit the sick
6. Visit the imprisoned
7. Bury the dead

Spiritual Works of Mercy

1. Counsel the doubtful
2. Instruct the ignorant
3. Admonish sinners
4. Comfort the afflicted
5. Forgive offences
6. Bear wrongs patiently
7. Pray for the living and the dead

As you can see, the Corporal Works of Mercy concern our help to people in need. How can I live in prosperity and peace if other people in the world are poor or suffering greatly? *(see Question 25)*. The Spiritual Works of Mercy have everything to do with evangelisation and the proclaiming of the faith, but also and especially with living my faith personally *(see Question 26)*. Our lives are not only intended for this earth (natural), but our ultimate destination is with God in heaven (supernatural). In this book you will see how the natural and supernatural sides of our existence both need attention for us to live life to the full as Jesus intended for us *(Jn 10:10)*.

Both the Corporal and Spiritual Works of Mercy are essential for Christians. They cannot be separated from each other. How can I pretend to wish my brother or sister the best by feeding them bread, without sharing with them the precious joy that I experience in my heart because of my relationship with Jesus? *(see Question 25)*. Let these Works of Mercy inspire you as you apply the social teaching of the Church in your daily life!

USING THIS BOOK

There is no need to start with Question 1 in this book: you can go directly to the question that interests you most. Every answer provides text and boxes that will help you deepen your understanding of the theme or continue your search for answers. This will also prevent you from being overburdened by the sheer amount of information. To get a global insight, you could start reading the principles of the social teaching of the Church *(see Basics)*. To deepen the answers you find in this book, it would be very good to discuss the theme with a small group, taking the text of the book as a starting point for your dialogue.

Scan

To further deepen your understanding of a theme, you can use two free apps with this book *(see page 15)*. The app ***Tweeting with GOD*** can be used to scan the main image just above the central question. This will lead you to an online synthesis of the answer and to many extra resources that can help you deepen the theme alone or in a group. The app ***Online with Saints*** can be used to scan the image of the saint that is related to the question. This will open a video and then their 'social media profile' in which the saint tells you about their life and experience.

Explore

The 'Explore' boxes give some more information about a theme. This can be closely related to the main question, or be a curiosity that helps you better understand the context. This fits with the entire idea of the book, which seeks to help you look at subjects from various angles and come to a personal conclusion, listening to both your faith and your conscience.

Read more

If you want to continue deepening your understanding of the theme, you can do so using the references to the following resources: *Catechism of the Catholic Church (CCC), Compendium of the Catechism of the Catholic Church (CCCC), Youth Catechism of the Catholic Church (YOUCAT), What to do? (DOCAT), Tweeting with GOD (#TwGOD), Online with Saints (#OnlineSaints).*

Pray

In prayer you relate to God, who created you. When you pray, you synchronise your heart and mind with his for a moment. That will change your entire outlook on things in daily life. It is very helpful to take time for prayer regularly. Praying is not always easy, but it can be learned *(see #TwGOD 3.1-3.8)*. The most important thing is your willingness to make time for God in your busy schedule, and to take a few minutes for being alone with him.

Quote

For every question one or more quotes from the teaching of the popes are offered. Reading these you can see that there is a continuity in their teaching. Every pope gave their own emphasis, but the social teaching of the Church is of all times. And in every time the Church helps to develop answers to modern questions, always in line with the fundamental teachings of Jesus.

Saint

You are not the first human being faced with such questions. Others have gone before you. Some of the people who in their faith and actions were very close to God during their life on earth, have been proclaimed blessed or saint. They are in heaven at this moment, where they are more than willing to pray for you. Their example can inspire you to become closer to God, and to involve him in every quest for answers.

Act

Often, there is not one single answer to a question. Much depends on the situation, and especially on the people involved. This book seeks to help you find general answers on the basis of the social teaching of the Church. Then it is up to you to apply the basic principles in your daily life. The examples and questions that are raised will help you think about these issues 'in advance' to help you get ready to face concrete situations. In your growing relationship with Jesus you can find real answers to real life issues.

Think

Where the 'Act' boxes help to consider one single theme a little more in depth, the 'Think' boxes help you continue your pondering even beyond what was said on these pages. As an individual reader, they help you to continue to develop your understanding and convictions. As a group, the questions in the 'Think' boxes can inspire you to speak together about the theme in search for possible answers.

Recap

In just a few words we give a concise summary of the highlights of the answer. The aim is not to be complete or comprehensive, but to help you see the essence of the answer and come to your personal synthesis of the theme. After all, it is you who will have to apply the principles of the social teachings of the Church in your daily life. What follows seeks to help you get ready for that task!

MORE READING

Tweeting with GOD *(#TwGOD)*

Frequent reference is made to *Tweeting with GOD*, where you can find answers to questions about God, the Church, prayer, and daily life. What started with a few questions by young people in one place, now is a comprehensive collection of tools to help people of all ages find answers to their questions. A brief answer can be found in the app, and a more complete version in the book ***Tweeting with GOD. #Big Bang, prayer, Bible, sex, Crusades, sin, career.*** Have a look at the website www.tweetingwithgod.com.

How to grow in faith

If after reading and discussing what follows on the next pages, you feel that you want to work with others in discovering more about the faith, you can use the book ***How to grow in faith. A life-changing course to explore the faith, search for answers or prepare for the Sacraments.*** It is a full course program for interactive meetings with suggestions of exciting group activities on a great variety of topics. Visit the website www.howtogrowinfaith.com.

Online with Saints *(#OnlineSaints)*

Every real life question in this book is linked to one of the saints. The saints were normal people like you, who stood out because of the extraordinary way in which they lived their lives with God and fellow human beings. Some of them were holy from the beginning, but most made many mistakes and committed sins before finally they discovered that nothing is more important than giving love the first place in your life. You can find many more saints in the app or the book ***Online with Saints. Discover friends and companions on your path to God.*** Check out the website www.onlinewithsaints.com.

www.tweetingwithgod.com

www.onlinewithsaints.com

BASICS

HOW CAN I CHOOSE WELL? WHAT IS THIS SOCIAL TEACHING OF THE CHURCH? WHAT ARE ITS PRINCIPLES?

The answers in this book are based on what we call the 'social teaching of the Church' or 'Catholic social teaching'. Basically, it is a modern interpretation of how to live your faith in daily life in relationship with other people and with God. It consists of a collection of principles which help us respond to modern day problems and situations. The social teaching of the Church is founded on and always in full accord with the teaching of Jesus in the Bible. It proposes principles for reflection, criteria for discernment and guidelines for action *(CCC 2423)*.

 # Acceptable for all

The social teaching of the Church is a guide to finding clear answers to very complex and often daunting questions. As it is founded on very basic human principles, much of it is acceptable even for people who adhere to a different or no religion: love, human dignity, solidarity... Such principles can be recognised in the Universal Declaration of Human Rights, for example *(see Question 13)*. All people will recognise such principles in the depth of their heart and conscience. The ultimate reason is that each of them has been created by God, and traces of his goodness exist in each of us. In this sense, the principles of the social teaching of the Church can be considered a gift to humanity, for they help to unearth the deepest truth about our being.

READ MORE

#TwGOD 2.45-2.46, 4.45 ; #OnlineSaints 1.3, 1.7.
Social teaching: CCC 2419-2425; CCCC 509; YOUCAT 438-439; DOCAT 22-25, 28, 34-36, 84-86, 104-105, 141.

 # Starting point

On these pages we present the most important principles of the social teaching of the Church. Mind you, these are intended as starting points for your reflection, and seek to help you formulate your personal answer to the complex questions and situations you may encounter in your life. It is therefore not a second set of Commandments *(see #TwGOD 4.9)*: rather, the principles of the social teaching assist you in living God's Commandments in daily life.

 # Customised answer

We can only deal properly with people when we see them as individuals, and not only as part of a group or community. As all people are different, our best course of action may differ between situations. That is why we propose not a rigid set of laws, but principles that will help you to formulate a customised answer to situations you encounter. The ultimate principle is not found in rules, but in love.

PRINCIPLES OF THE SOCIAL TEACHING OF THE CHURCH

Love – *The double commandment*

Love of God and neighbour is the most fundamental principle of Christian teaching. It is based on the words and example of Jesus himself, who demonstrated that God is love *(1 Jn 4:16)*. He taught us the summary of all God's commandments in the double commandment: **1**. 'Love God with all your heart, with all your soul, and with all your mind;' **2**. 'Love your neighbour as yourself' *(Mk 12:29-31; see #TwGOD 1.19)*. Each of the next principles seeks to help you realise this double commandment of love.

Human dignity – *Right to life, freedom and work*

Human dignity is the intrinsic value of people created in the image and likeness of God and redeemed from their sins by Jesus *(see #TwGOD 1.26)*. Human life is a precious gift and infinitely desired by God, the creator *(Gen 1:26)*. This gift needs to be protected and promoted so people can live their lives in full as Jesus wants for us *(Jn 10:10)*. Every human life is precious, and no one can claim the right to dispose of the life of another, however small or fragile. On the contrary, the freedom to live needs to be promoted. Work is an important way in which people can realise their human dignity. Discrimination, slavery, inhumane working conditions, and everything that reduces the apparent value of individuals and groups is contrary to human dignity.

The common good - *The earth is of us all*

The common good is the totality of social conditions that allow a person to achieve their communal and individual fulfilment. The beauty of the earth and its fruits belong to all its inhabitants *(Gen 1:28-30)*. We have been created for living together with others. God intended us to be one single family, one body with many members, where we are all brothers and sisters *(1 Cor 12:12-13)*. Pope Benedict XVI explained: "Besides the good of the individual, there is a good that is linked to living in society: the common good. It is the good of 'all of us', made up of individuals, families and intermediate groups who together constitute society" *(Caritas in Veritate, 7)*. Every individual is called to work for the promotion and realisation of the common good.

Solidarity - *Option for the poor*

Solidarity means sharing the material and spiritual goods fairly among all people. "How does God's love abide in anyone who has the world's goods and sees a brother or sister in need and yet refuses help?" *(1 Jn 3:17)*. God has a preference for the small and weak *(Lk 10:21; 1 Cor 1:27)*. Jesus described how, after our earthly life, we will be judged on the basis of our faith and what we did for the hungry, thirsty, homeless, naked, sick, and imprisoned *(Mt 25:31-46)*. The Christian 'option for the poor' means that we choose to share our gifts and resources with our brothers and sisters, first of all with the poor and vulnerable.

Care for creation - *Our common home*

Care for the environment is very Christian. After the creation of the world, God entrusted it into our care *(Gen 1:28)*. It is our common home: he gave us the earth as a gift, a gift that does not belong to any individual or group, but to humanity throughout the ages. Therefore, a just division of the fruits of the earth among people is in order. It also means that all together we have to take care of our common home. As Pope Francis asked: "What kind of world do we want to leave to those who come after us, to children who are now growing up?" *(Laudato si', 160)*.

Justice and peace - *Living together*

Justice searches for what is right, and leads to peace. It is more than a just application of the laws that regulate our harmonious living together as human beings. Clarity and charity go hand in hand. True justice is always connected to love which is the highest form of justice, and God's very being *(1 Jn 4:8)*. Justice for all is closely related to solidarity with the poorest, a just division of resources, and even to the protection of the environment for the good of all. Only when this is realised can we grow towards peace on earth which is very close to God's heart *(Lk 2:14)*.

Subsidiarity *– Shared responsibilities*

The principle of subsidiarity aims at a just division of tasks and responsibilities with human dignity and the participation of everyone in mind. 'Subsidiarity' comes from the Latin word for 'help', *subsidium*: only when this help is needed should a higher social authority come to assistance. Subsidiarity regulates society's activities in such a way that individuals and local communities are best supported in their daily lives. What individuals can accomplish by themselves should not be done by the community. And what a family or local community can do should not be done by higher government. For example, you could leave decisions to the lower level if the most accurate information is available there, but might need to involve higher government so that global aspects can be taken into account.

Participation *– In family and society*

Each of us is called to contribute to the community according to the personal gifts we have received from God *(1 Cor 12:4-11)*. We should all participate as members in the social, economic and political life of our families, communities and societies *(see Question 20 & 21)*. The aim of every participation is to serve the common good of all. The way we participate is based on solidarity and subsidiarity: care for the weak and vulnerable should go hand in hand with a just division of tasks and responsibilities. Society needs good Christian leaders, politicians, health carers, cleaners, food producers, artisans, merchants, religious guides...

Evangelisation *– Sharing your joy*

Our relationship with Jesus is something very precious. Whatever happens, you may be certain that he is with you and loves you, even if you have difficulty in recognising his presence or in believing in him. His love and presence is such great and joyful news that you cannot keep it only for yourself. Jesus asked us to share our faith with others and let them know how a life with God changes the outlook of human existence *(Mk 16:15-16)*. This evangelisation starts with the way in which you yourself live your faith, and continues with the way you speak about God in your own words. When your Christian lifestyle and words correspond with each other, you are greatly contributing to the evangelisation of your peers.

Integral human development *– The orchestra of life*

Integral human development means that we should help others not just by caring for their stomach or physical safety but by keeping in mind everything that makes them into a human person, including their faith *(Mt 4:4)*. All the principles of the social teaching together help to promote an integral development of the earth and its inhabitants. As Pope Francis said, "human life is like an orchestra that sounds good if the different instruments are in accord and follow a score shared by all" *(4 Apr. 2017)*. To accomplish this, we need to take care of every community member and their personal development in all dimensions: physical, spiritual, intellectual, emotional, social... Only then can we further develop our communities and work for the common good.

YOUR
NEIGHBOUR
IS GOD

POVERTY & SOLIDARITY

Should I give money to a beggar?

How can I respect the dignity of the needy? Should I give without questioning? Why does God not act?

Jesus said: "It is more blessed to give than to receive" *(Acts 20:35)* and: "Give to everyone who begs from you" *(Mt 5:42; Lk 6:30)*. Charity includes freely giving of your time, talents, and possessions to others without expecting anything in return *(Lk 14:12-14)*. There is but one condition: that you do so out of love. Saint Paul said it very poignantly: "If I give away all my possessions… but do not have love, I gain nothing" *(1 Cor 13:3)*.

Jesus taught us the double commandment, which is the ultimate answer to all questions in this book: **1**. 'Love God with all your heart, with all your soul, and with all your mind;' **2**. 'Love your neighbour as yourself' *(Mk 12:29-31; see #TwGOD 1.19)*. "God loves a cheerful giver" *(2 Cor 9:7)*, Saint Paul said, one who gives freely and without reluctance. God does not want you to give out of a sense of duty, but out of love. When you freely give something to those in need, try to do so out of love for God and your fellow human beings. Do not worry! God knows our love is often imperfect, and that consequently also our giving is imperfect. Most of us will still feel some attachment to what we give away or some reluctance to help. But that does not stop God from loving us!

Why doesn't God act?

This is how God acts to help the poor: through you! So, do not say: 'God does not act', but let your minds, hands, and possessions be his to use and share! Take a real look around you. In your own environment there are people and situations where your help is needed. So, roll up your sleeves and get busy! Your contribution can be financial aid, manual volunteering work, or simply your listening ear and friendly face. All of this is charity. Of course, you cannot responsibly give away that which you need to support those who are in your care. But there is so much you *can* give *(see Explore)*.

Human dignity

When you give to someone in need, do so always in a way that respects their dignity. Human dignity is a fundamental principle of Christian life *(see Basics)*. You are not superior because you happen to have something you can give away! Your life has no more value or dignity than that of any other person. Every human life is sacred, because each of us is desired and created by God. Pope Francis invited us to ask: "Am I able to stop and look in the face, in the eye of that person who is asking me?" *(9 Apr. 2016)*. Offering a simple coin in haste without looking at the person or without stopping to talk is no real charity.

Solidarity

A further principle for our lives as Christians is solidarity *(see Basics)*. "The many situations of inequality, poverty and injustice, are signs not only of a profound lack of fraternity, but also of the absence of a culture of solidarity," Pope Francis said *(1 Jan. 2014)*. Solidarity by giving our time, energy, resources, and possessions to someone can help them to lead their life with dignity. At the same time, through our sharing we realise our own human dignity, which is not made to be lived alone, but in solidarity with others! Saint John the Baptist said: "Whoever has two coats must share with anyone who has none; and whoever has food must do likewise" *(Lk 3:11)*. So, maybe true solidarity means that you share so much that you and the other are equally poor (or rich)...

READ MORE

#TwGOD 1.34-1.35, 4.45; #OnlineSaints 1.45, 2.8.
Poverty & Solidarity: CCC 2443-2449 & 1939-1942;
CCCC 520 & 414; YOUCAT 448-451 & 332;
DOCAT 164-170, 238-241 & 100-103.

EXPLORE

Is giving money and food all we can do?

For those who have it, sharing money or food is a great way to show true solidarity with the hungry. And you can help in many more ways. Both short term emergency relief and long-term solutions are needed. There are some great innovative examples by young people. In Zimbabwe, a boy founded a start-up business by employing those most in need of a job. A girl from Jordan set up a training project for women and disabled people to generate an independent income. In Australia young people set up a mobile washing service for those on the streets, and constructed shower vans, for example. So, even if you cannot give money or possessions, your energy, mind, and merciful spirit can change the lives of people forever!

PRAY

God, lover of the poor, help me to give and share what you have given me with the needy in love, solidarity and respect. Help me to be less selfish and possessive.

To give or not to give

When a child asks for a venomous snake or a bear as a pet, would its parents not refuse in order to keep their child from harm? As in every aspect of life, discernment is needed in relation to when, how and what you give. Sometimes the principal rule of love prevents you from giving what would be harmful to the other person or if your donation might be abused. At the same time, you will want to respect their freedom of choice and dignity. It is good to think about these questions in advance *(see Act)*. Finally, *when in doubt: give*. Do not be afraid to get it wrong: "It is more blessed to give than to receive" *(Acts 20:35)*.

THINK

- Have you ever given money to someone in need? Would you do it again? Why (not)?
- Have you ever talked to a homeless person? How can you treat people in need with love and respect?
- Do you think that helping the needy indeed should be a priority for Christians? Why (not)?
- Are there any people who need help around you? What can you do?

QUOTE

Our preferential option for the poor

"The needs of the poor must take priority over the desires of the rich; the rights of workers over the maximisation of profits; the preservation of the environment over uncontrolled industrial expansion; production to meet social needs over production for military purposes."

[Pope John Paul II, To Christian communities, 14 Sept. 1984, 5]

"God shows the poor 'his first mercy'. [Inspired by] this divine preference… the Church has made an option for the poor… This option – as Benedict XVI has taught – 'is implicit in our Christian faith in a God who became poor for us, so as to enrich us with his poverty'… Without the preferential option for the poor, 'the proclamation of the Gospel, which is itself the prime form of charity, risks being misunderstood or submerged by the ocean of words which daily engulfs us in today's society of mass communications.'"

[Pope Francis, Evangelii Gaudium, 198-199]

SAINT

Why doesn't God help poor, hungry, and thirsty people?

Vincent de Paul was a French priest who saw the needs of the poor. It is thanks to him that we have the great work of the Saint Vincent de Paul Societies. He felt that it was his calling to be God's instrument and help the poor in their difficulty. He also taught them to help each other and see how God loved each of them. God also wants you to be his instrument. Are you ready?

ACT

Should I give money to a homeless person?

The answer depends on the situation. You want to help improve the life situation of this person. That is a great cause, for he or she is a child of God! Whether you decide to give money or not, engage with the person in front of you and treat them with dignity, respect, and love. The following considerations may help.

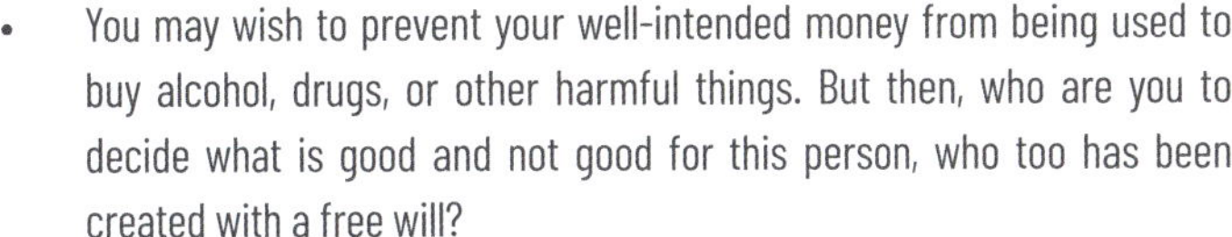

- You may wish to prevent your well-intended money from being used to buy alcohol, drugs, or other harmful things. But then, who are you to decide what is good and not good for this person, who too has been created with a free will?
- Giving food instead of money can be a genuinely good solution; if possible, let them tell you what food they prefer, and what their dietary needs are. But people need more than food alone *(Mt 4:4)*: money is needed for night shelter, personal hygiene, clothes...
- Unfortunately, the exploitation of beggars, of children, of handicaps is quite common in certain places: your donation may end up in the pockets of undeserving patrons of this modern-day form of slavery. But if you do not give, they may be punished for not having collected enough. But then again, your money allows for the continuation of a cycle of abuse...
- In many places there are (church) charities that deal with these dilemmas every day and have found good solutions; you could decide to give through these organisations. But elsewhere, charities cannot reach everyone or cannot be trusted 100%; then you had better give directly to the person in the street.

As for many of the questions in this book, it is ultimately up to you what you decide in your heart. Let love be your guiding principle, rely on your conscience and the help of the Holy Spirit, and you will choose well! *(see #TwGOD 4.1)*.

RECAP

When in doubt: give! Always give with attention to the human person in front of you who has exactly the same worth as you. God needs you to act!

2

I cannot help everyone; where is the limit?

What is charity? How much should I give?
Why is the Church so rich? Is my money used well? What if I am poor?

Poverty & Solidarity

A great way not even to get started is by thinking of everything that is impossible. Whatever the situation, you are bound to compose a long list! And yet, the Bible teaches: "Nothing will be impossible with God" *(Lk 1:37)*. Jesus never tells us to limit our charity, and he even invites to do the impossible, like he did when feeding over 5,000 people with five loaves and two fishes! *(Jn 6:3-13)*.

A first answer to the question can be found in the community: no individual can end all poverty, but the entire world population can! You are but a part of something much bigger. True, even if you were to work 18 hours a day you could not feed all the hungry in the world. However, your vocation is not to solve all global problems (unless you become pope or secretary general of the United Nations). Your task is much closer to home.

What did Jesus say?

Jesus said that at the Last Judgement he will stand before all people of all times to separate the blessed from the cursed. The blessed are those who did something for people in need. In reality they did it for Jesus: "I was hungry and you gave me food, I was thirsty and you gave me something to drink, I was a stranger and you welcomed me… Just as you did it to one of the least of these who are members of my family, you did it to me" *(Mt 25:35-36.40)*.

We form one family with all the people in the world, sharing the same Father in heaven. Then how can we let some of our brothers and sisters starve while we are enjoying a reasonably good life? You cannot say you are a Christian if you do not share what you have with others. The more people embrace Jesus' invitation, the better a place to live the world will become. This is yet another reason for the importance of evangelisation! *(see Question 26)*.

Charity

God is love *(1 Jn 4:8)*: you exist only because of his 'charity', another word for love! Charity is every act of love that helps advance the wellbeing of your fellow human beings. Think of food for the poor, education for the young, shelter for the homeless, evangelisation for the unknowing... Think also of visiting your old and lonely neighbour, bringing some warm soup to that woman on the street corner, looking after the children of that poor family while the parents are at work...

Bonus

And there is a bonus: no act of charity will remain completely without reward: "Give, and it will be given to you", Jesus said *(Lk 6:38)*. Still, we should not give in order to receive back. On the contrary, Jesus asks you to give in secret, and not even 'let your left hand know what your right hand is giving' *(Mt 6:3)*. God the Father sees what you are doing, and whether you do it for yourself or out of love for him and your neighbour. He will 'reward' you in secret. That is between him and you. For now, your duty is to give.

READ MORE

#TwGOD 2.7, 4.46; #OnlineSaints 1.47, 2.19-2.20.
Charity & Distribution: CCC 1822-1829 & 2401-2406; CCCC 388 & 503-505; YOUCAT 309 & 426-427; DOCAT 6-7, 14-16, 27 & 89-94, 237.

EXPLORE

A rich Church?

Some people find a convenient excuse for not donating to the Church or other charities by saying that these institutions are so rich or will not use the money well *(see #TwGOD 2.7)*. Unfortunately, it is true that sometimes painfully spared donations to charity were abused by people for their own wealth and sumptuous life style *(see #TwGOD 2.13)*. Thankfully these are exceptions, although as a community we should watch carefully and eradicate all abuse.

Most of the 'wealth' of the Church is in the infrastructure and land of schools and churches, hospitals and other charitable institutions, sometimes housed in monuments that are maintained at high cost as cultural heritage. Cultural heritage is not just something of the past, but is relevant at this moment. Through their beauty, architecture and art honour God the creator, just as did the people who offered money for their realisation. Their possible high economic value exists only on paper: if they were sold (you can only do this once!), the care for orphans, homeless, sick, elderly and uneducated would not be possible any more.

PRAY

Dear God, help me to see how your charity embraces me and those in need alike. Help me to be generous without counting, while taking responsibility for those in my care.

Too poor to give?

It is up to you to discern how much you should give away of your wealth, time, and talents *(2 Cor 9:6-7)*. Just remember Jesus' words: "From the one to whom much has been entrusted, even more will be demanded" *(Lk 12:48)*. There is always something you can share. When Jesus observed a poor widow donating two small coins, he complimented her because she gave of what little she had and not of her abundance like the others *(Lk 21:1-4)*. Even if you live (partly) off charity, you probably still can share something with others. In fact, often poor people are the best in sharing, and an example to us all!

THINK

- Have you ever been in a situation of poverty? Do you sometimes give to charity? Why (not)?
- Would jobs for everyone solve poverty? Does poverty cause crime? How?
- Are there more important issues than poverty for Christians? If so, which?
- Would you pay more taxes if this were to eliminate poverty? Why (not)?

QUOTE

Charity with the poor

"One cannot experience charity without having interpersonal relationships with the poor: living with the poor and for the poor. The poor are not numbers but persons. Because by living with the poor we learn to practise charity with the spirit of poverty; we learn that charity is sharing. In reality, not only is charity that fails to reach the pocket a false charity, but charity that does not involve the heart, soul and our entire being is a concept of charity not yet fulfilled."

[Pope Francis, To Caritas Internationalis, 27 May 2019]

SAINT

Should I give everything away?

Most of us are not called to give everything away like Saint Francis did *(see Question 8)*. In fact, several saints were very rich. Take Saint Louis, King of France. He did a lot of charity, both financially and with his own hands. He did not spend excessive money on himself or his family, but rather spent it on many good causes. The remainder of his fortune he passed on to his son, as he felt was his duty as a king.

ACT

How much should I give?

The biblical custom was to give away at least 10% of your income *(Gen 14:20; Deut 14:22-24)*. Why ten? It is enough for you to feel it, but usually not so much that it would lead you into severe difficulty. If everyone were to give 10% it would make a real difference. That said, giving 10% is probably not enough: look at the number of people living without the bare necessities of life. So, how much should you give?

- Instead of asking 'what is enough?' you could ask 'how much can I give?' – knowing that every act of charity means a smaller or greater sacrifice from your side. But are the poor not suffering more than you?
- Ask yourself: do I give enough in comparison to what I spend on myself beyond the basic needs? Do I really need that costly takeaway coffee every day? Or can I give that money to charity? Do I drive a big car because I need it, or just as a status symbol? Do I really need to go out so much?...
- There is no problem in spending some money on a good party from time to time. In fact, Jesus emphasised the importance of celebrating *(Lk 15:10.23)*. But like everything, we should do so within reason and with moderation *(Mt 9:15; see #TwGOD 4.10)*. How can you do this?
- Jesus said: "It is easier for a camel to go through the eye of a needle than for someone who is rich to enter the kingdom of God" *(Mk 10:25)*. Could it really be a calling from God to live in extreme wealth while others cannot buy the basic necessities of life? Can this wealth be put to some advantage of others, like an estate employing those in need of work?

- Do you reserve something special for Sundays or feast days, while being more moderate during the week? Would that improve your enjoyment on Sundays? Could this be a simple way to save some money for charity?

The idea is not to give so much away that you yourself end up in a situation of need, especially when you have to care for a family. So, be careful with your discernment, but do so with a generous heart.

RECAP

Do not ask how much you must give, but how much you can give! Charity is all about sharing people's lives, not just money. The Church uses her possessions to do just that.

We cannot welcome all migrants, can we?

Is it not better to send them back and help there? Shouldn't we rather search for long-term solutions?

Poverty & Solidarity

'Jesus was a refugee', Pope Benedict stated firmly *(see Quote)*. The social debate about welcoming refugees and migrants is very heated. For Christians the answer should be simple: welcoming strangers is a profound Christian duty *(Heb 13:2; Rom 12:13)*. It is like welcoming Jesus himself! *(Mt 25:35)*. We absolutely need to look for long-term solutions for problems that cause migration, but meanwhile, what do we do for the people at our borders?

Biblical duty

The Bible teaches: "You shall love the stranger as yourself, for you were strangers" *(Lev 19:34)*. Most modern populations come from immigration long ago. The first humans probably came from Africa, many Americans were originally refugees from Europe, many Australians descend from people who were forced to leave Ireland and England, within Europe and Asia people have migrated throughout the ages. Many of them were genuine refugees fleeing poverty or war, some came as cruel conquerors *(see #TwGOD 2.34)*.

As Christians we know that we are refugees in a religious sense too, exiled from paradise as "poor banished children of Eve", in the words of the *Salve Regina* hymn *(see #TwGOD 1.4)*. The world is our temporary dwelling place, a "valley of tears" until we are ready to enter eternal life with God in heaven *(see #TwGOD 1.50)*. Meanwhile, we are asked to treat each other as brothers and sisters, sharing with those who have less than us. So, there are many reasons to welcome migrants and refugees in our countries.

True solidarity

Human dignity and solidarity are two cornerstones of Christian life *(see Basics)*. But do we always build our lives on these stones? True solidarity means that you have to be ready to give up something of yourself: some space, some habits, some wealth... *(see Question 1)*. Theoretically, eventually there will be a turning point when it is no longer as interesting to migrate because the prospects in your country are similar to those in the country of origin. Only then will we have achieved full solidarity! For Christians, true richness is found in the closeness to God and fellow human beings. The aim is not for all to become poor, but that all will be rich in a Christian sense, close to God and each other. Solidarity and evangelisation are both great ways to get there *(see Question 25 & 26)*.

Here or there?

It sounds so sensible: let us help our fellow human beings in their own country so they do not have to leave their homes. If it works, this is a very good solution – as long as it is done for the right reasons. Beware of the moral pitfall: do you suggest this because you want the best for these people, recognising their human dignity, or because you do not want to be annoyed by their presence? Unfortunately, such a solution is no option for many refugees who are forced to flee their homes and countries because of violence, persecution, and war. Their future depends on our hospitality.

READ MORE

#TwGOD 1.3, 1.5, 2.50; #OnlineSaints 2.24.
Dignity & Freedom: CCC 1699-1709 & 1730-1742;
CCCC 358 & 363-366; YOUCAT 280 & 286-290;
DOCAT 47-56, 63-66 & 106.

EXPLORE

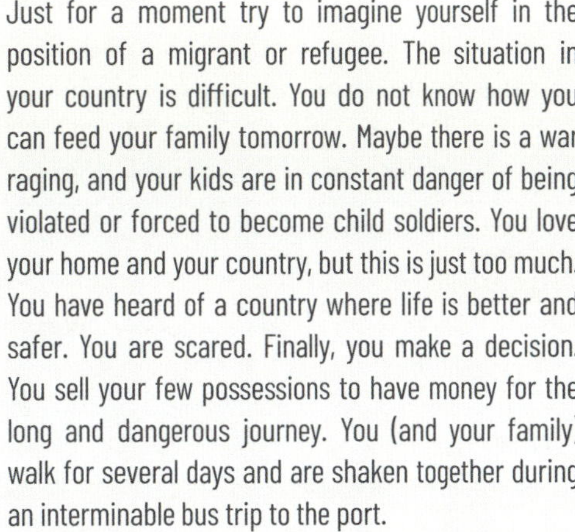

It could have been me!

Just for a moment try to imagine yourself in the position of a migrant or refugee. The situation in your country is difficult. You do not know how you can feed your family tomorrow. Maybe there is a war raging, and your kids are in constant danger of being violated or forced to become child soldiers. You love your home and your country, but this is just too much. You have heard of a country where life is better and safer. You are scared. Finally, you make a decision. You sell your few possessions to have money for the long and dangerous journey. You (and your family) walk for several days and are shaken together during an interminable bus trip to the port.

After a long search, you find a ship at an exorbitant price. The small open boat is overloaded with people in situations similar to yours. The journey overseas starts well, but then the weather changes. A child playing near the side falls overboard and drowns. There are hardly any provisions. You are all at the end of your strength and then... a ship! The crew sees you but the ship turns away. The law in their country does not allow them to help you. When you finally disembark at your destination you are taken into custody and locked up. Is this the promised land you dreamed of?

PRAY

Dear Lord, so many people are suffering in terrible conditions. Help me to stand ready for those who need my help and welcome strangers with a warm heart.

Segregation is discrimination

'That physician is welcome, but not her unschooled sister.' Segregation or selection at the gate is a terrible thing. We rightly take a strong stance when people or groups are being discriminated against in our societies *(see Question 12)*. We should do the same when it comes to welcoming refugees. Jesus does not say that we should welcome only those who can be useful to us! For him the life of a doctor, nurse, or engineer has exactly the same value as that of someone with less education. The problem is the same if you say you want to help exclusively Christian refugees. The persecution of Christians is a terrible thing, and we should do much more to prevent it – but just as terrible is the persecution of people of other religions.

QUOTE

Welcome strangers!

"The globalisation process can be an opportunity... if the unequal distribution of the world's resources leads to a new awareness of the necessary solidarity which must unite the human family... The Church... works so that every person's dignity is respected, the immigrant is welcomed as a brother or sister, and all humanity forms a united family."

[Pope John Paul II, World Migration Day, 2000, 4-5]

"Jesus' parents were also obliged to flee from their country and seek refuge in Egypt, to save the life of their child: the Messiah, the Son of God was a refugee... The purpose, the destination of humanity's great journey through the centuries: to form one family, with, of course, all the differences that enrich it but without boundaries, recognising each one as a brother or sister."

[Pope Benedict XVI, Angelus, 16 Jan. 2011]

"We often hear it said that, with respect to relativism and the flaws of our present world, the situation of migrants, for example, is a lesser issue... [For] a Christian... the only proper attitude is to stand in the shoes of those brothers and sisters of ours who risk their lives to offer a future to their children. Can we not realise that this is exactly what Jesus demands of us, when he tells us that in welcoming the stranger we welcome him? (Mt 25:35)."

[Pope Francis, Gaudete et Exsultate, 102]

SAINT

From refugee to monk

Moses the Ethiopian was a highwayman. He was a savage brute and easily enraged. When he had to flee from government troops, he asked refuge in a monastery deep in the desert. The porter was afraid and wanted to turn the big man with his cruel face away, but the abbot opened wide the door to welcome this stranger. Eventually Moses became intrigued by the monks' lifestyle and asked to join them.

THINK

- How do you define 'home'? Does everyone have the right to such a home? Why (not)?
- Do you know any immigrants? Do you know any people who have emigrated from your country? What is the difference?
- How would you help an immigrant learn your local language? What can Christians do for refugees?
- Should immigrants have the same rights as native citizens? Why (not)?

ACT

Stop, we are full! Or are we?

How many refugees and migrants can we comfortably welcome in our country? The answer is probably many more than you think. Here are some thoughts.

- How much space does a person need to live in? The answer will be different if you ask in a crowded city or in the countryside. So how can you be sure when your country is 'full'? Whom should you ask?
- If you were to choose whom to let in, how would you do this? Women and children only? That would mean disrupting families. Skilled workers first? That would be discrimination. The Christian principle of the absolute value of human life may help. If you really have to choose, choose those who are in most imminent danger first. But what will you do for the others?
- Have you ever visited a refugee camp? In many cases, living conditions are extremely bad. Is it humane to let people live in such circumstances instead of letting them into our countries, even if that would mean some setback for us?

Finally, you have worked hard for what you have, so why should you give it away to others? But for a moment place yourself in their position, knowing that all you need is some help to get started. What would your advice to yourself be?

RECAP

Welcoming strangers is a Christian duty. As is helping people where they are, far away or at our doorstep. Searching for long-term solutions should not keep us from helping now.

How far should migrants integrate in society?

How can we react to 'religious invasion' and 'migrant violence'? Can we turn away economic migrants?

There are various causes that make people want to migrate. Indeed, refugees in danger need to be helped urgently. But is that an excuse not to help the so-called 'economic migrants'? Many of them lived in deplorable situations at home. And that brings us back to the principle of solidarity *(see Basics)*. Jesus said that when we welcome a stranger in need, we welcome himself! *(Mt 25:35)*.

Social changes

In your society, some people will emigrate to take up a job in another country. Similarly, people from less-developed areas in the world may wish to search for a job in your country in the hope of a better living standard for themselves and their family. Are they to blame for this? Those who say 'They take our jobs', forget that many jobs they do not wish to do are done by immigrants: cleaning, garbage collection, dirty jobs... Does a person from your country really have more right to a particular job than someone who was not born there?

It is good to help people where they are, where they are at home *(see Question 3)*. But if they desire to move, is that not their private choice? From a Christian viewpoint, there is no problem if society changes culturally as a result of immigration. Whatever our origin, together we form God's family of brothers and sisters. By reflecting God's love in our lives and receiving his grace together, we can find the right path also when many immigrants come our way.

Freedom

There is no such thing as absolute freedom *(see Question 13)*. Wherever people interact, we need regulation. Even the docile monks of Saint Benedict asked their founding father to write a monastic rule to help them live together in a Christian manner *(see #TwGOD 2.25)*. The laws of our nations foresee something similar. Everyone, also immigrants, needs to follow the law

EXPLORE

Religious invasion and violence?

You sometimes hear people complain about a 'religious invasion' under the guise of migrants and refugees. Some would be paid handsomely to contribute. Even when this is true for some, can we therefore refuse to help all migrants and refugees, or accept only the Christians among them? The best answer to a 'religious invasion' is to (re)discover our own faith, living and sharing it with conviction in today's society. The principle of religious freedom includes the right to evangelise and share our religion with others. A right that we should use more as Christians, as long as we leave the individual free to respond according to their hearts *(see Question 26)*. A purely Christian society does not exist, but we should be free to live and announce our faith just like everyone else.

However, not everyone does so peacefully. Religious freedom is great, but should we really tolerate a religion which promotes violence or inequality? Pope Francis said in Egypt: "We have an obligation to denounce violations of human dignity and human rights, to expose attempts to justify every form of hatred in the name of religion, and to condemn these attempts as idolatrous caricatures of God" *(28 Apr. 2017)*. These words are directed to everyone, migrants included.

of the country. Sometimes the law gets it wrong, though. For example, when it violates fundamental human rights, like that of freedom of religion *(see Question 23)*. If people wish to wear the traditional dress of their religion, should they be allowed to do so? How is that different from a Catholic nun who wishes to wear her habit in public?

Criminals?

It is a widespread human flaw to blame a group for what individuals do. With all the emphasis we place on the individual and personal responsibility, this is a very unchristian thing to do. If there are radicalised warmongers among migrants, they need to be stopped promptly. If there are criminals among refugees, they need to be tried with justice – and attention to the degree of guilt: when someone who is hungry steals some cereals to feed their child, then an unjust society rather than the person is to blame. Jesus told us to accept that sometimes weeds may sprout up among the good wheat *(Mt 13:29-30)*. The biblical answer to the problem that among genuine refugees there may be some abusers is not to close our doors but to carefully make the weed harmless.

READ MORE

#TwGOD 2.1; #OnlineSaints 2.43.
(In)equality & Migration: CCC 360-361, 1934-1942; CCCC 68, 412-414; YOUCAT 61, 330-331; DOCAT 58-60 & 248-250.

PRAY

Father, help me to welcome people in need, leaving them free to be themselves as created by you. Inspire me to gently share the beauty of my faith.

House rules

Do you welcome your guests unconditionally? There are probably certain house rules you would like them to follow. You will also allow them a good amount of liberty so they feel at home away from home. It is not much different for questions related to the integration of immigrants in society. Like everyone, the newcomers will have to comply with the law. But they will also need help and understanding as they learn about a law and customs which possibly are very different from what they were used to. Learning the local language can be very difficult for some. Is that a reason to turn them away? Integration and inculturation are important. But should people give up their own language and culture? Inculturation can be a two-way process, in which all can learn something new *(see Quote)*.

QUOTE

Integration is not assimilation

"Integration is not... an assimilation that leads migrants to suppress or to forget their own cultural identity. Rather, contact with others leads to discovering their 'secret', to being open to them in order to welcome their valid aspects and thus contribute to knowing each one better. This is a lengthy process that aims to shape societies and cultures, making them more and more a reflection of the multi-faceted gifts of God to human beings. In this process the migrant is intent on taking the necessary steps towards social inclusion, such as learning the national language and complying with the laws and requirements at work, so as to avoid the occurrence of exasperated differentiation...

In our society, characterised by the global phenomenon of migration, individuals must seek the proper balance between respect for their own identity and recognition of that of others... The way to take is the path of genuine integration with an open outlook that refuses to consider solely the differences between immigrants and the local people... Christians cannot give up proclaiming the Gospel of Christ to all creation (Mk 16:15)*. Obviously, they must do so with respect for the conscience of others."*

[Pope John Paul II, World Migration Day, 2005, 1-3]

SAINT

A holy slave and migrant

Bakhita was brought to Europe from Africa as a slave. She had no particular training or skill. Still, she was welcomed warmly in a monastery in Italy, where the sisters protected her against her 'owners'. She adapted to the way of life of the sisters and took her religious vows, but also brought some freshness to the convent through her way of living the faith.

THINK

- To what extent has your culture become richer through immigrants?
- Do you think there is a relationship between immigration and crime? Why (not)?
- Is it Christian if the government gives better houses to immigrants than to local poor?
- Should the government limit the number of immigrants? What is a good number? Why?

ACT

Integration or cultural diversity?

You may have heard how the Queen of England once received a head of state with an exquisite banquet. On the lavishly laid table there were finger bowls for the discrete purification of fingers between courses. The conversation was flowing nicely until everyone held their breath with a gasp and indignant faces. Unknowingly the visitor had committed a shocking break with etiquette by drinking from his finger bowl... Only the Queen kept her cool. She calmly picked up her own finger bowl and sipped from the lukewarm and slightly dirty water. A possible diplomatic incident was averted. More importantly, the honour of her guest was saved!

- Instead of the heated debate on whether, how, and when to welcome migrants and refugees, maybe we can learn from this example to be courteous with a cool head. With time some of their customs may be considered a welcome fresh wind.
- Something similar may happen to you when you are welcomed in an Asian country where chopsticks are customary at table. But probably your attentive host will quietly slip a fork next to your plate! How can you apply this to the theme of integration and cultural diversity?
- Have you ever wondered how migrants see the society in which they have arrived? Whether they are happy to be here? Whether they feel at home? How strange some of your customs are to them? How many things they were accustomed to they miss?

The Church helps people where they are, without discrimination. In faraway countries, and also nearby in our societies. Immigrants who need help can count on her attention too. What can you do to assist your local church in this effort?

RECAP

Integration is a two-way process, enriching for both host country and immigrants. Everyone should get a fair chance, but whoever misbehaves must be corrected.

YOUR
NEIGHBOUR
IS GOD

ENVIRONMENT & ANIMAL RIGHTS

5

Why should I care about the environment?

Must I believe in climate change? How is this linked to solidarity? Should we look for a new planet?

Noticing that technological and economic development seem the only things that really matter in our society, Pope Paul VI spoke of 'integral human development', which 'aims at the development of each human being and of the whole person' *(Populorum Progressio, 14; see Basics)*. Jesus wanted us to live life to the full *(Jn 10:10)*. We should keep a keen eye on all aspects of human life: social, economic, political, technological, cultural, environmental, relational, personal, spiritual... Such a 'holistic' approach to the human person is not new – for example it lies at the basis of most Catholic education, which has a long history. The notion of integral development is related to much of what is said in this book. When speaking about the environment, Christians search for integral ecology, never forgetting the social and human dimensions.

Ecological conversion

Several recent popes have called for an 'ecological conversion' *(see Question 25)*. Pope Francis defined this as "a transformation of hearts and minds... to overcome problems such as hunger and food insecurity, persistent social and economic distress, the degradation of ecosystems, and a 'culture of waste'" *(8 June 2019)*. Care for 'our common home', the planet as created by God, is connected to many other important social issues, and an essential duty for all Christians. This includes fighting global warming or climate change. Scientists are still discussing exactly how much of this is caused by human activity and how much by natural variation, but it is very clear that our wasteful way of living has an important impact on the environment. And that the first victims of climate change are the least wealthy.

How is this Christian?

'The ecological debate is primarily political and ideological', you sometimes hear. However, there are compelling reasons for Christians to get involved. The Bible warns that if the destroyers of the earth do not repent, they will be destroyed

EXPLORE

Is the end near?

Prophets of doom say that if humanity is to survive, we need to find another planet soon. Obviously, that would be the height of the 'waste culture': throw away the old planet and find a new one… But is it really too late? Looking at certain predictions it would seem so. However, nature often has proved to be more resilient than predicted. And Jesus taught us that it is never too late to turn around from our deviations: God is always waiting for us *(Lk 15:20; 2 Pt 3:9)*. So why not all pull together in a huge effort to bring about change? God created the world for us, and he will never let us go down with it. Hope is a very Christian virtue *(Heb 6:18)*. If we start now, it is not too late!

themselves *(Rev 11:18)*. This destruction takes many forms. When God made the world, he paused regularly and "saw that it was good" *(Gen 1:10)*. He then entrusted dominion and responsibility for all creation to us people *(Gen 1:28-30; 2:15)*.

As 'stewards' we can take from nature what we need for our lives, but we are also to care for creation *(see #TwGOD 4.48)*. The earth is like a vineyard entrusted to us to cultivate the best fruits possible *(Mt 21:33-41)*. It is given into our care, but we cannot claim ownership. Everything is made and held together in Jesus alone, so if we abuse the earth, we abuse Jesus! *(Col 1:16-17)*. Conversely, caring for creation means caring for something God loves very much.

 # Solidarity

Is it really fair that less than one quarter of the world population consumes 80% of the global resources? *(FAOSTAT)*. Is that our idea of a fair sharing of God's gifts of creation among our brothers and sisters? *(see Question 1)*. The integral development we are called to strive for includes all humanity, so something has gone severely wrong here *(see Question 9)*. Only solidarity, first of all with the poorest in the world, can solve this great injustice.

When enforcing much-needed measures to protect the environment, these measures should be imposed in all severity on the richest countries, to leave some space for further development of other countries. Obviously, this cannot be done without affecting the economy. Remember, solidarity involves giving something up for the sake of the other… In Christian terms this is considered progress, for life in society as a whole will be improved. This gives us a foretaste of heaven on earth *(Lk 17:21)*.

READ MORE

#TwGOD 4.36, 4.48; #OnlineSaints 1.36.
Care for creation: CCC 2415; CCCC 506;
YOUCAT 436; DOCAT 256-269.

PRAY

Dear God, I thank you for the gifts of creation.
Help me to protect and share these in
global solidarity, with a keen eye on the
integral development of every individual.

Make a difference

Saint Francis was greatly in love with God. Consequently, he also greatly loved people, animals, and all God had created *(see Question 8)*. Through his words and simple lifestyle he proclaimed the Christian message of love and hope. Imagine that he would have sat back and sighed: 'Oh what the heck, what difference will it make on a global scale anyway?' Thankfully he did not. By doing simply what he could, he has had a lasting influence on generations of people for over 800 years now. You may not think of yourself as a new Saint Francis, but you definitely can make a difference! *(see Question 6)*.

QUOTE

For all humanity

"By an ill-considered exploitation of nature [humanity] risks destroying it and becoming in his turn the victim of this degradation… This is a wide-ranging social problem which concerns the entire human family. The Christian must turn to these new perceptions in order to take on responsibility, together with the rest of men, for a destiny which from now on is shared by all."

[Pope Paul VI, Octogesima Adveniens, 14 May 1971, 21]

"The danger of serious damage to land and sea, and to the climate, flora and fauna, calls for a profound change in modern civilization's typical consumer life-style, particularly in the richer countries… The world's present and future depend on the safeguarding of creation."

[Pope John Paul II, World Day of Peace, 1 Jan. 1999, 10]

"Can we remain indifferent before the problems associated with such realities as climate change, desertification, the deterioration and loss of productivity in vast agricultural areas, the pollution of rivers and aquifers, the loss of biodiversity, the increase of natural catastrophes and the deforestation of equatorial and tropical regions?" **[Pope Benedict XVI, World Day of Peace, 1 Jan. 2010, 4].**

SAINT

Prayer, responsibility, and action

Pope Paul VI spoke prophetic words at a time when most people were not yet aware of the global impact of the way we treat the environment *(see Quote)*. He can be called the first modern pope, with great attention to the new and complex questions raised by our times. His response was one of prayer, taking responsibility, and call to action.

THINK

- Are you worried about global warming? How is this Christian? What can you do?
- What lessons can be learned from nature and global crisis?
- Who should take first responsibility for pollution, individuals or the government? Why?
- Do you think global solidarity between peoples or nations is really possible? How?

ACT

How can I contribute?

Christian solidarity demands a drastic redistribution of resources globally. The living standards of the rich simply cannot be upheld morally if we take human dignity seriously. What can you do yourself?

- Overconsumption is a big issue. Jesus warned against such excesses *(Lk 12:15)*. Will you change your furniture every few years, or maybe just give it a lick of paint? Is repairing an option instead of buying new? What can you give up?
- Sometimes a boycott of particularly wasteful or polluting products can contribute, especially when the entire community joins in. What products you use now fall into this category? And while we are in your pantry, which products can you replace with eco-friendly alternatives?
- By buying local products you stimulate local farmers and avoid long-distance transportation. But if these are produced in green-houses using a lot of energy this advantage is lost. So you may have to adapt your menu further and use especially seasonal products. This brings you closer to the natural cycles of a time to plant and a time to reap *(Eccl 3:2)*.
- Travelling greatly impacts the environment, and seemingly contradicts the biblical admonition not to pollute the land *(Num 35:34)*. Can you travel less? How can you compensate for the impact of necessary travelling?

Searching further, ideally with friends or family, you will find other questions, but also new ways to live your life and faith in a more ecological way right now. Whatever you do, do not forget to pray – and to take care of your neighbour as well!

RECAP

God created our 'common home', so we can all grow together with an integral attention for all aspects of life and faith. Christians should preserve our planet for the good of all.

Why is wasting food and water such a great sin?

How important is recycling and renewable energy? What if I cannot afford an eco-friendly lifestyle?

Is recycling Christian, you can ask. Well, if the earth and everything on it is a present from God to us all, we are very ungrateful and lack love for the giver if we throw his gifts away, spoil, or hoard them for ourselves alone *(1 Pt 4:10)*. Integral ecology means that we have an eye for the wellbeing of everyone and everything. Jesus invited us to let our gifts and our light shine for the good of all and the glory of God *(Mt 5:16)*.

Looking at things globally, it is clear that a redistribution of resources and opportunities is in order. We can start making a real difference by choosing products that are made with recycled material rather than with freshly mined raw materials. And use renewable energy sources like the sun, the wind, the waves… Although this may be a little more expensive at times *(see Act)*, we could consider it an investment in our Christian duty to care for God's creation, our common home *(see Question 5)*.

A community impact

You may say: mine is but a small contribution, what impact does it make? But it is a contribution nonetheless! And if more members of the community join in, the impact is largely multiplied. After all, the world numbers over 2 billion Christians, almost a third of the world population. Imagine the impact we can have on the world if we all recycle and use renewable energy wherever we can! If then we add to that various ways of showing more solidarity with our brothers and sisters who are less fortunate, we are truly contributing to the world becoming a better place. But it does start with your personal contribution!

Industrial food waste

Globally, about a third of all food that is produced is never eaten and goes to waste *(FAOSTAT)*. During the various stages of production and delivery a part is lost because of carelessness,

EXPLORE

Towards zero waste

Our food is God's gift, fruit of the earth and work of human hands, as the priest says at Mass. In our homes the waste factor should be zero. It should deeply hurt us to throw out even a small scrap of good food. There are various methods that can help prevent your veggies going to waste behind other groceries in the fridge: from moderate shopping to inventory apps, or talking fridges that keep perfect track of your ingredients and expiry dates. Actually, that expiry date is a great indicator, but also a cause of food waste. You can easily learn to recognise how products are often good to eat even after that expiry date.

That leftover from dinner can serve as tomorrow's lunch, a snack, a basis for your soup, or together with some other leftovers as a 'review-of-the-week-dinner'. It is deeply biblical to let nothing go to waste, not even the crumbs that fall under the table *(Mt 15:26-27)*. And when food has sadly gone to waste, think about how you throw it out. As compost the produce of the earth can return to being fertile earth itself.... Leading a more ecological life as a Christian should start here and now, with the preservation and consumption of all our food, letting nothing go to waste of God's good gifts.

overproduction and commercial choices, for example. And do you know how much food is thrown away in a supermarket so that they can provide you a varied choice of fresh food until evening? Food banks and soup kitchens are great examples of integral ecology in that they feed the poorest and most hungry, often with food that otherwise would go wasted. Many of these initiatives were started by Christians.

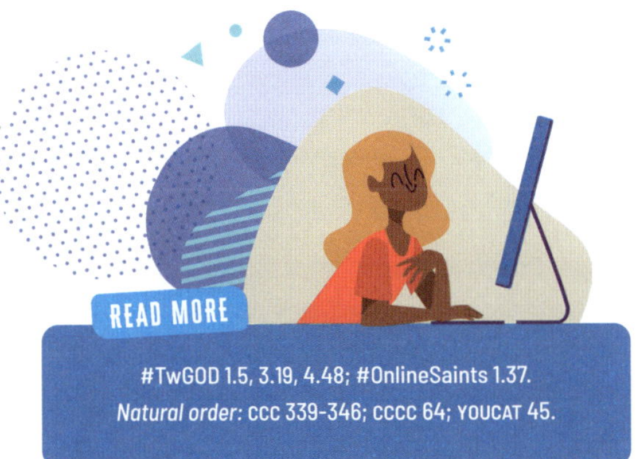

READ MORE

#TwGOD 1.5, 3.19, 4.48; #OnlineSaints 1.37.
Natural order: CCC 339-346; CCCC 64; YOUCAT 45.

 # Wasting food a sin?

It is in fact very Christian to fight the sin of food waste. "Let nothing be wasted", Jesus said after having fed 5,000 people *(Jn 6:12)*. How could he let the food given by his Father be thrown out? It should be the same for us. The parental admonition: 'Finish your plate because children far away are dying of hunger' sounds a little comical, for how is cleaning my plate here tonight going to soothe hunger there? But the idea behind it is very important: the more we waste here, the less resources are available for others globally. That is why Pope Francis said that we steal from the poor when we throw out food *(5 June 2013)*.

PRAY

Lord of heaven and earth, you entrusted the stewardship of the world to us. Help me to limit my use of resources, fight every form of waste, and improve my sharing with others.

The blue gold

Water is fundamental for every form of life, so it is a sin to spill it. Alarmingly, about a third of all people in the world do not have access to clean drinking water even today *(WHO 2019).* And clean water is becoming rarer. Look at the rivers, lakes, and even oceans that are polluted by human action. There is a great danger in the fact that water becomes ever more the 'blue gold': the first to suffer under its scarcity are the poorest, and the powerful will fight over it just as they do over other natural treasures. As Christians, it is through the water of Baptism that we receive new life in Jesus. Holy water reminds us of that essential moment. We have a sacred duty to prevent precious water being spilled or spoiled, and to promote access to it for every person in the world. What can you do yourself?

QUOTE

Human ecology

"The importance of ecology is no longer disputed. We must listen to the language of nature and we must answer accordingly. Yet... there is also an ecology of man. Man too has a nature that he must respect and that he cannot manipulate at will. Man is not merely self-creating freedom. Man does not create himself. He is intellect and will, but he is also nature, and his will is rightly ordered if he respects his nature, listens to it and accepts himself for who he is, as one who did not create himself. In this way, and in no other, is true human freedom fulfilled."

[Pope Benedict XVI, To the Bundestag, 22 Sept. 2011]

"We have grown indifferent to all kinds of wastefulness... A decline in birth rate, which leads to the aging of the population, together with the relegation of the elderly to a sad and lonely existence, is a subtle way of stating that it is all about us, that our individual concerns are the only thing that matters. In this way, 'what is thrown away are not only food and dispensable objects, but often human beings themselves.'"

[Pope Francis, Fratelli Tutti, 18-19]

SAINT

Finding God in creation

As a native American, Kateri Tekakwitha lived in harmony with nature, using what she needed without excessive damage to the environment. She used to find God in the forest, where she placed small crosses to indicate how he is present everywhere in his creation.

THINK

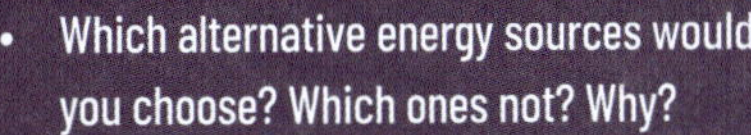

- What are some things which you recycle? Why? Can you do more?
- Do you sometimes throw out food? Do you want to change this?
- Which alternative energy sources would you choose? Which ones not? Why?
- Do you think people could make a living from picking-up garbage? Is that a good thing?

ACT

Can I afford to live in an eco-friendly way?

There are many things each of us can do without excessive spending. The following points may help you get some ideas.

- Seasonal products take less energy to produce. They usually are cheaper too. Bringing your own bag means one single-use bag less to recycle. What other simple actions can you think of?
- Don't forget to think about water. You are surely trying to avoid bottled water already to prevent plastic waste. Did you think about reducing your showering time, or not letting the tap run while you brush your teeth? What simple things can you do to preserve water for the sake of your brothers and sisters in Christ?
- The amount of waste plastic we accumulate daily in an average household is enormous. What can you do to reduce this? And how can you reduce your energy use? Did you think of using less heating or cooling, for example? Or driving a little slower?
- Separating your waste may seem tedious, so turn it into an opportunity for prayer: pray an Our Father every time you are struggling to make nice bundles out of your paper or plastic waste, for example.
- How often do you choose to buy recycled products? Food waste has been mentioned also in these pages. What else can you do?

Most of this is not unique to Christians. However, we should be very motivated to investigate these and more ways to contribute concretely to preserve God's great gift of the creation, which we have been given in custody by God.

RECAP

It is a Christian duty not to waste the resources and fruits of the earth. We can all do something. Integral ecology includes solidarity between rich and poor.

Was Jesus vegan?

Should Christians be vegetarian? Does care for creation include a vegetarian diet? Why were animals sacrificed in the Bible?

There are a good number of reasons to eat less meat, including animal welfare, the high price, the huge amount of energy and resources needed to produce it, the impact on the environment, health issues... But are there any biblical reasons? In the Bible, the eating of meat is considered normal. God told Noah: "Every moving thing that lives shall be food for you; and just as I gave you the green plants, I give you everything" *(Gen 9:3)*. So people are conceived as omnivores. In the desert, God fed his people bread in the morning and meat in the evening *(Ex 16:12)*. Still, not all meat was intended for human consumption. For example, the Old Testament considered pork meat unclean *(Lev 11:7-8)*.

Jesus the omnivore

On the eve of the great escape from Egypt, God commanded that every family should slaughter, prepare and eat a lamb. To remind them of God's saving grace, they were to celebrate this every year at the Passover *(Pesach)* feast by eating a lamb with bitter herbs *(Ex 12:3-14)*. Jesus celebrated Passover with his disciples *(Lk 22:8)*. He also ate fish *(Lk 24:41-43)*. So, he clearly was neither vegan nor vegetarian. He said that all food was to be considered clean: everything could be eaten, including pork *(Mk 7:15-19)*. For Jesus, impurities rather come from the hearts of people...

Vegetarian Christians?

God does not command vegetarianism or veganism. But a good case can be made for moderation in eating animals. Saint Benedict ordered a mainly vegetarian diet for his monks *(see Saint)*. Monastic orders like Trappists, Trappistines, and Carthusians strictly abstain from meat and at times even dairy items. Saint Francis loved animals as his brothers and sisters – but was not a vegetarian *(see Question 8)*. However, in his fasting and sharing he sought to be moderate, also when eating meat and fish. In conclusion, there is no need to feel guilty if you enjoy an occasional Sunday roast. At the same time, adhering to the Christian tradition of moderation and fasting by making more vegetarian choices can have a great effect on your spiritual life, a fairer distribution of goods, the environment...

No quarrels

Saint Paul stated that there should be no quarrelling between those who prefer meat and those who eat only vegetables *(Rom 14:1-4)*. He ate meat, but also said that he would rather abstain from meat than lead others into sin *(1 Cor 8:13)*. The debate between vegetarians and meat lovers should be a gentle one. Christians are called to strive together for an integral ecology *(see Quote)*.

The concern for animals and nature is inseparably connected to issues like a fairer global distribution of food, wealth, and opportunities *(see Question 1-4)*. Remember, God created all the earth for our wellbeing, and confided his creation into our care. If we have to choose between letting people die of hunger or feeding them meat, for example, we have to choose the latter. But if in the 'production process' of our daily slice of meat, precious food is being fed to animals instead of to the hungry, the Christian answer should be moderation or even abstinence from meat *(see Act)*.

Sacrificing animals

The animal sacrifices that God asks for in the Old Testament seem barbaric to our modern minds. But in a way, animals are 'sacrificed' for our wellbeing also today: for food, clothing, shoes, medication... *(see Question 8)*. At least these sacrifices serve a useful purpose. But why the seemingly pointless animal sacrifices in the Bible?

You could consider them as a reminder of the horror of sin! The animals were sacrificed or chased into the desert as a 'scapegoat'. This was done to atone for the people's sins and make their relation with God possible once more *(Lev 16:6-10; #TwGOD 1.19)*. Blood is a sign of life, and sprinkling with blood cleansed people of their sins - which otherwise would bring about death *(Ex 24:4-8)*. These bloody and horrific remedies demonstrate how terrible sin is *(see #TwGOD 4.13)*. Jesus changed all this when he said: "I desire mercy, not sacrifice" *(Mt 9:13)*. He broke once and for all with the custom of animal sacrifices: he offered himself as the ultimate sacrifice on the cross *(Heb 10:14-18)*.

READ MORE

#TwGOD 1.3, 1.7, 3.19, 4.1, 4.9, 4.11; #OnlineSaints 2.9. *Conscience & Natural law:* CCC 1749-1754, 1776-1794 & 1949-1960; CCCC 367, 372-376 & 415-417; YOUCAT 291, 295-298 & 333; DOCAT 57 & 12, 217.

PRAY

God our creator, you entrusted the care for every living being to us. Help me to make careful choices so I can respect and care for your creation also in what I eat.

Beans on Wednesday?

Wednesdays and Fridays are traditional Christian days of fasting. The Catholic tradition of eating fish and abstaining from meat on Fridays can take a whole new dimension. Not only is it a healthy spiritual practice to remind yourself of Jesus' suffering on Good Friday *(see #TwGOD 3.19 & 3.31)*, but also an ecological choice. Of course that is less the case when you substitute your meat with fish that is in danger of being overfished…

A good case could be made for introducing a vegetarian Wednesday. Judas betrayed Jesus on a Wednesday. With every selfish choice you make during the day, however small in your eyes, you join in his betrayal. As a reminder and a small sacrifice to show how important Jesus is for you, you could opt for a vegetarian or vegan menu on Wednesdays. Even if you do not consider this a sacrifice, it will still remind you of your choice for Jesus.

QUOTE

Co-worker of the creator

"If, with regard to natural resources, especially under the pressure of industrialisation, an irresponsible culture of 'dominion' has been reinforced with devastating ecological consequences, this certainly does not correspond to God's plan… [The] famous words of Genesis entrust the earth to man's use, not abuse. They do not make man the absolute arbiter of the earth's governance, but the creator's 'co-worker': a stupendous mission, but one which is also marked by precise boundaries that can never be transgressed with impunity."

[Pope John Paul II, Jubilee of the agricultural world, 11 Nov. 2000, 4]

"Saint Francis (see Question 8)… shows us just how inseparable the bond is between concern for nature, justice for the poor, commitment to society, and interior peace. Francis helps us to see that an integral ecology calls for openness to categories which transcend the language of mathematics and biology, and take us to the heart of what it is to be human."

[Pope Francis, Laudato si', 10-11]

SAINT

A monastic diet

Benedict of Nursia made his monastic communities settle permanently on a plot of land, and – next to their prayer life – work the earth in harmony with the cycles of nature: *ora et labora* (see #TwGOD 2.9). A diet of mainly vegetables and dairy products was complemented with an occasional bird or fish – no meat from four-legged animals.

THINK

- 'Feeding everyone in the world is more important than my steak.' Do you agree?
- If creation carries in itself traces of God, what can people learn from the animal world?
- Animals eat other animals, so why should we become vegetarians?
- Should restaurants be obliged to offer a choice of vegetarian and vegan dishes? Why (not)?

ACT

Why be (more) vegetarian?

Christians have good reason to lean towards a more vegetarian diet. While there is no biblical ban, you can ask whether it is morally permissible to eat meat and fish abundantly.

- About a third of all available land, a third of all grain, and a sixth of all clean water is used for raising livestock *(FAOSTAT)*. The 70 billion animals raised annually for human consumption lead to more emissions than the world's transportation fleet of cars, trucks, planes, and ships together. To this should be added the pollution generated by the production and transportation of whatever these animals eat. How does this relate to our Christian duty of being stewards of creation?
- Most meat comes from factory farming and industrial slaughter. Its low prices come at the expense of quality, animal wellfare and environmental impact. But meat is still expensive in comparison to vegetables. Many people cannot afford ecologically produced meat. Should they be allowed to buy industrial meat after all, lest meat becomes a privilege of the wealthy? Or would the Christian solution be to eat less meat altogether?
- Overfishing leads to heated political debates, but is also an attack on the ecosphere. Think of the damage to the seabed and ecology by trawls and dynamite, for example. Is it still morally permissible to eat fish from the ocean? And actually, how sustainable is farmed fish actually?

There is a difference between celebrating Sundays and feast days with an occasional steak, and insisting on your right of a daily portion of meat. Can a Christian in good conscience eat such expensive food every day? Even when knowing the impact on the environment and human health?

RECAP

If a (more) vegetarian or vegan diet helps feed more people in the world, this is a very Christian option! Jesus was not vegan, but put an end to animal sacrifices.

Is it so bad if pandas go extinct?

What if wild beasts are attacking civilisation?
Are there limits to animal rights?
Should indigenous people continue to hunt?

Poaching and deforestation of bamboo led to the late 20th century cry for saving the giant panda which was on the verge of becoming extinct. The good news is that there is hope for pandas: a huge package of preservation measures is showing the first signs of success. This is a great example of how human beings can exercise their stewardship of God's creation *(Gen 1:28)*. However, other species too are greatly endangered because of human intervention and climate change, including rhinos, red tunas, polar bears, certain bees... And then there are different plants that are on the verge of extinction, diminishing ecological diversity.

Disappearing species

How bad is it from a Christian viewpoint if these species disappear? Jesus said that God loves and cares for the birds of the air and the lilies of the field. He added that in the eyes of God we are even more valuable, and that he wants to provide for everything we need *(Mt 6:26-30)*. If species disappear through natural causes, this is sad but part of the course of nature. However, if humans are the cause of the extinction, we need to take our responsibility in protecting the creation that has been entrusted into our care. How painful it is to realise that we are destroying the beauty of God's creation by our way of living, in particular when this could be changed quite easily!

Does God care?

Animal welfare may not be a recurring topic in the Bible, but that does not mean that it is unimportant to God. Rather, the proper treatment of animals by good people is presupposed: "The righteous care for the needs of their animals" *(Prov 12:10)*. Those who keep animals are told to keep track of the condition of their flocks, and provide for their needs *(Prov 27:23)*. The commandment 'not to muzzle the ox when it is treading the grain' seems to be but a gesture of kindness towards the beast *(Deut 25:4)*. It would be cruel not to let it eat a little of the food it is processing as a reward *(1 Cor 9:9-10)*. Although animals like sparrows may not have a high value in the eyes of people, God forgets none of them! *(Lk 12:6)*.

Not at every price

Sometimes we experience a clash between the welfare of human beings and that of animals. Jesus is clear: even if animals are desired, created and fed by God, and therefore should be cared for, human beings are of more value *(Mt 6:26)*. They should be fed and cared for first *(Mt 15:26-27)*. If ferocious wild beasts are threatening villagers, catching and displacing the animals can be a good solution. But if the threat can only be taken away by killing them, this needs to be done *(1 Sam 17:34-35)*. On the other hand, we should strive to live in harmony with nature. Is it reasonable that we move into the domain of beasts, and then kill all of them to protect ourselves?

READ MORE

#TwGOD 1.19, 1.48, 4.36, 4.48; #OnlineSaints 1.36.
Care for animals: CCC 2416-2418;
CCCC 507; YOUCAT 56-57, 437; DOCAT 49, 264.

EXPLORE

Hunting for food

Although animals have rights as creatures of God, these are subordinate to fundamental human rights. Take the example of indigenous peoples who for many generations have lived off the forest or the land. They do not hunt on an industrial scale, and usually have a great respect for the balance between species in nature. Would it be moral to force them into another way of life and forbid them to hunt – even if the view on animal welfare and hunting may have changed in other parts of the world? Or can you drive these people out of a reserve which was instituted long after their ancestors arrived on the land in order to protect a certain species against extinction?

People have a natural right to live off the earth, and to live in harmony with all creation. Remember God's words to Noah: "Every moving thing that lives shall be food for you" *(Gen 9:3)*. In the Western world, hunting for food is not strictly a necessity, but there are other reasons for hunting, like culling to keep a good balance between the various species. Too many animals of one kind could destroy the local ecosphere. As such, hunting can be part of our role of being stewards of the earth.

PRAY

Dear God, creator of people and animals, help me to care for all creatures, protecting and preserving them, while not forgetting the primary importance of people in your eyes.

Useful animals

Watchdogs, packhorses, milkcows, there are plenty of examples of animals being useful for us. We should be grateful and reward the beasts by treating them well. After the fall into sin of the first people, God clothed them in animal skins *(Gen 3:21)*. Animals can be used to serve the wellbeing of human beings. But human dignity must be upheld. Cruelty and unnecessary suffering of animals is contrary to our dignity *(CCC 2418; #TwGOD 1.48)*. Sometimes, animals are used for very dangerous, but very useful operations. Think of dogs looking for people in debris after an earthquake or sniffing out landmines that could have exploded when a child stepped on one. Or think of how medical test animals or the transplantation of their organs help to save human lives *(see #TwGOD 4.36, 4.40 & 4.48)*. If they die in the process, that is sad, but they died for a great cause. In our just striving for animal welfare, we should not deprive animals of their purpose, which includes their usefulness to people *(Gen 1:27-28; 3:21)*.

QUOTE

Beneficiaries and stewards

"[Humankind] has the right to dispose at will of non rational beings, plants or animals (which does not free him of the obligation that he has before God, and in keeping with his own dignity, to avoid unnecessary brutality and cruelty), but he does not possess this right over other men or subordinates."

[Pope Pius XII, To the World Medical Association, 30 Sept. 1954]

"We human beings are not only the beneficiaries but also the stewards of other creatures. Thanks to our bodies, God has joined us so closely to the world around us that we can feel the desertification of the soil almost as a physical ailment, and the extinction of a species as a painful disfigurement. Let us not leave in our wake a swath of destruction and death which will affect our own lives and those of future generations... 'An incredible variety of insects lived in the forest and were busy with all kinds of tasks... Birds flew through the air... How can fish swim in... rivers which we have polluted? Who has turned the wonderworld of the seas into underwater cemeteries bereft of colour and life?'"

[Pope Francis, Evangelii Gaudium, 215]

SAINT

Preaching to the animals

Among the saints, Francis of Assisi is a classical choice when speaking about the environment. World animal day is celebrated on the 4th of October because it is his feast day. He loved animals, preached to them, but also ate them when meat or fish were offered to him in answer to his begging for food.

THINK

- Do you think people can become too attached to their pets? Should we feed people before pets?
- Would you visit a zoo? Should we free animals that have been in captivity all their lives? Why (not)?
- Should hunting as a sport be forbidden? Is there a Christian way to look at this question?
- If medical tests on animals can save human lives, should this be permitted? Why (not)?

ACT

Protecting animals

Care for animals is an important Christian duty, but how far should we go?

- At the creation, God intended the world to be good, but then came the fall into sin, which altered it *(see #TwGOD 1.2 & 1.4)*. In the future life with God, animals will no longer prey on each other *(Isa 11:6-9; see Question 26)*. What could this mean for us now?
- Mosquitoes are very irritating and do not seem to serve a real purpose. It might seem better to exterminate them altogether. But then, why did God create them in the first place?
- Why should we be allowed to keep pets, is it not better to let these animals wander around freely in nature?

Saint Anthony of Padua preached to the fish, Saint Francis tamed a wolf, and Saint Agnes took her name from lambs (*agnus* in Latin). There are great examples of saints taking a stance for animal welfare. But then, Saint Gall sent away a bear, Saint Patrick chased snakes from Ireland, and Saint Hubert is the patron saint of hunters. All these saints address a different theme. What can you learn from them?

RECAP

We need to do what we can to prevent animals going extinct because of our doing. Our survival takes precedence, for human beings are more important than animals.

Is population growth wrong?

What is this 'integral ecology' really?
Is true sustainability possible? Should I ditch my phone?

The beauty of the oceans and their deep blue expanse, the great ecological diversity of creation with its colours, faces, and uses, and the vastness of the (rain) forests with all their medicinal and other riches are the great treasures of creation as we have received it from God: together with the unfathomable depths of the human being they are all interrelated in one global ecosphere. It is an imperfect foretaste of the perfect life that awaits us in heaven. Jesus said that God does not forget one of his creatures *(Lk 12:6)* and to announce the Gospel to all creation *(Mk 16:15)*. This is the basis of the Christian idea of integral ecology, which searches to promote the common good of all and everything *(see Basics)*.

Man, beast, plant and stone

Integral ecology considers the ecology of people, beasts, plants, and stones in themselves and in relation to the entirety of creation. The chaos theory as hypothesised by Lorenz states that in apparently random and chaotic mathematical systems an underlying pattern can be observed. Integral ecology wants to consider the underlying pattern that shows how all that preceded and will follow is interconnected, and created by a loving God who calls us to action. Therefore, rather than an economic crisis, a social crisis, or an environmental crisis, there is one global crisis in which everything is interconnected. The only way to find sustainable solutions to this crisis is by an integral ecology in answer to God's love.

Population growth

After creating the world and human beings, God told us: "Be fruitful and multiply, and fill the earth" *(Gen 1:28)*. It is natural for a man and a woman to leave their family to get married and start one of their own *(Mt 19:5)*. At the same time, every new human being that is born has an impact on the environment which God told us to take care of... Some people think it is selfish to have children for this reason.

Note, however, that you would not be here if your parents had thought in that way. It is painful to see how rich countries are sometimes pushing birth control strategies in poorer areas of the world *(see Quote)*.

Birth control?

In the Catholic perspective, human sexuality is much more than a survival of the species. It is a deep experience of the loving unity between a married man and a woman. Their love is open to new life, which may come forth from every sexual act. However, this does not mean that we should give in to a blind procreation. The Catholic view on a just birth control through natural methods *(see #TwGOD 4.25)* must be considered within the total framework of an integral ecology. Neither abortion nor artificial contraception can provide the answer *(see #TwGOD 4.23 & 4.28)*. Nor can government pressure.

Only the future parents have a right to discern in prayer and conscience how many children they can responsibly maintain in this world: "Let them thoughtfully take into account both their own welfare and that of their children, those already born and those which the future may bring... Finally, they should consult the interests of the family group, of temporal society, and of the Church herself" *(Gaudium et Spes, 50)*. Measures to enforce a reduced population growth often emerge from a selfish mindset. As Pope Francis said, if rich countries would consume a little less of the global resources, there would be enough for all, including the newly born *(Laudato si', 50)*.

EXPLORE

A Meccano ecosystem?

The construction toy Meccano came into being during the industrial revolution, when young people saw Eiffel tower-like steel constructions of strips and bolts everywhere. Contrary to much of the industrial development, it proved to be a very sustainable toy, made of durable material with which you can create and recreate endless new constructions. At the end of its life cycle the steel can be melted and given a new use.

When well designed, the constructions are strong enough to stand on their own, and can reach great heights. But loosen a few bolts and the entire thing collapses. The same is true for the ecosystem, in which the life cycles of species are interrelated and interdependent. Maybe Meccano can help to discover what integral ecology really means.

READ MORE

#TwGOD 3.19, 4.25, 4.48; #OnlineSaints 2.37.
Birth regulation & Globalisation: CCC 2368-2373; CCCC 497-498; YOUCAT 418-421 & 446-447; DOCAT 129-130 & 229-234, 242-247, 251-255.

PRAY

Dear God, you call us to an integral view of ecology. Help me to strive for the wellbeing of every human person, animal, and all of created nature.

Sustainable... but not!

Take a country which outsources all heavy industries to low-income countries in order to lower national emissions. Or one that compensates for emissions by planting trees in another country, claiming land that could have been used for development. Is this sustainable development? On a local level you would say yes, but considered globally the problem is only displaced to areas where people already have to face many disadvantages with respect to established economies. Yes, rich countries in particular should take measures to protect the environment. But the goal does not automatically justify the means. Only an integral view of ecology is able to unearth such miscalculation on a global level, and come up with globally sustainable alternatives.

THINK

- Is everything interconnected in our world? If so, what does this mean?
- What are the consequences of population growth? Are these connected to issues like global warming?
- What factors (should) motivate people to want or not want children? What does this mean?
- How would you define sustainable ecology? And what is integral ecology in your words?

QUOTE

Solidarity or international pressure

"The more fortunate should renounce some of their rights so as to place their goods more generously at the service of others... Without a renewed education in solidarity, an overemphasis of equality can give rise to an individualism in which each one claims his own rights without wishing to be answerable for the common good." [Pope Paul VI, Octogesima Adveniens, 23]

"At times, developing countries face forms of international pressure which make economic assistance contingent on certain policies of 'reproductive health'. Yet... demographic growth is fully compatible with an integral and shared development. To blame population growth instead of extreme and selective consumerism on the part of some, is... an attempt to legitimise the present model of distribution, where a minority believes that it has the right to consume in a way which can never be universalised." [Pope Francis, Laudato si', 50]

SAINT

Family and children

Zélie and Louis Martin did not get married with only procreation on their mind. In fact, both had seriously contemplated entering celibate religious life. Still, they considered the children that were the 'fruit' of their intimate relationship as gifts of God. Four of their children died, and the five others all entered religious life.

ACT

Ban my phone?

Your smallest device takes a great amount of energy and carbon footprint to develop. It also uses ever rarer resources like gold and terbium, that are mined at great cost and damage to nature. The working conditions of the miners are often not very good. These materials and the devices need to be transported all over the world. Also the data centres that keep wifi and cellular networks in the air use a lot of energy. So, if you want to express your care for creation as a Christian, should you ditch your mobile phone? After all, every life includes some suffering... A few thoughts along the lines of integral ecology.

- Your existence and everything you do takes energy. By making certain choices you can reduce this. But you cannot avoid having a certain impact, with or without a phone. There is no need to feel guilty about this: God knew this when he created you!
- You are here on earth to interact with other people. If you need a phone to do so, then it fulfils a vital function. Can you fully operate as a social human being in this world without it? If not, how can you help the other half of the population to get connected?
- That said, you could opt for a phone that is easier to recycle and is made of recycled material. Thus you make less of a claim on the resources God gave for everyone to enjoy.
- You can decide to change your phone less frequently, and maybe only have the battery replaced when that is draining too quickly.
- And at the end of its life cycle, you offer the device for recycling, of course. This not only reduces the need for excavating more raw resources, but also it creates some jobs for the people who take them apart.

This example shows how integral ecology has an impact on all areas of daily life.

YOUR
NEIGHBOUR
IS GOD

JUSTICE & PEACE

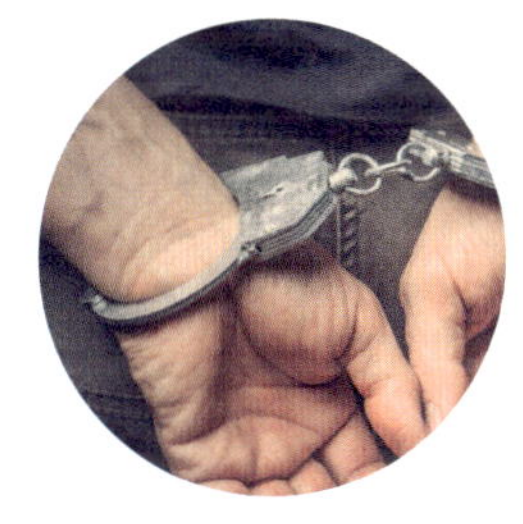

10

Is modern justice different from biblical justice?

Why doesn't the good guy always win?
Are charity and justice related? Is reporting a crime betrayal?

Justice & Peace

When animals kill each other, and even their own, we usually say that this is the course of nature. But we do not accept a similar behaviour in people, and cry for justice when a human being attacks or murders another. There is a fundamental difference between animals and people *(see #TwGOD 1.3)*. God made us in his own image *(Gen 1:26-27)*. You are God's child, his son or daughter.

Just as every artist puts part of themselves into their artwork, so there are traces of God's own being in us. That alone makes every human being extremely valuable, worthy, and irreplaceable: God destined us for a life that will continue into eternity. Consequently, every person has the right to everything they need to live out their full potential – always in just solidarity with others *(see Question 1)*.

God's justice

Justice and peace for all should be our constant concern as Christians. "The Lord is a God of justice" *(Isa 30:18)*. Justice is part of God's being: he is just and cannot be unjust. Justice simply means 'what is right'. In the Bible, righteous people are those who behave in a way to God's liking. The opposite of what is right is sin. Our sins bring us far away from God, and make our relationship with him very difficult. To repair this relationship, our sins need to be taken away.

We can never justly repay the great damage caused by our sins, so we are doomed – unless God shows another part of his being, which is love. God is love *(1 Jn 4:8)*. Not a pink and fluffy fairytale love: God's love is real, and sometimes even tough. Just like life on earth. God's justice is always in line with his love: he is merciful in his justice. Therefore the Bible implores us to return to God and "hold fast to love and justice" *(Hos 12:6)*. Made in God's likeness, we too are called to live in love and mercy.

Revenge, justice, or mercy?

When we say 'I want justice!', we often mean that we want revenge. Although this is understandable, it is not good: "Never avenge yourselves… 'Vengeance is mine, I will repay, says the Lord'" *(Rom 12:19)*. God's 'revenge' is different from ours. He does not want to get even with someone by punishing them (retributive justice): he wants them to change their ways (restorative justice) *(see Question 11)*. It seems just that if you punch me, I have the right to punch you back. The Old Testament law said: "Show no pity: life for life, eye for eye, tooth for tooth, hand for hand, foot for foot" *(Deut 19:21)*. But Jesus corrected this and taught us not to repay evil for evil *(Mt 5:38-44; Rom 12:17)*. We should indeed hunger and thirst for justice, but always with mercy as our utmost desire *(Mt 5:6-7)*.

Justice and peace

Christian justice goes beyond what our judicial systems can achieve. For God, the ultimate answer is mercy, not the just application of the law. Justice alone cannot change the world and make it a better place: only love can. Justice and mercy go hand in hand, you cannot have one without the other. As Christians we are called to mercifully strive for a just division of resources, goods and opportunities, promote reconciliation, and work together for a world in which everyone lives in peace with each other. This is not just an ideology, but will become ever more a reality as more people adhere to the simple principle of love for God and neighbour!

EXPLORE

Why not the good guy?

The law should be applied objectively and impartially. Thankfully, this often is the case. But sometimes the good guy does not receive justice because of flaws, faulty defence, unjust laws, discrimination, corruption, crime… Our judicial systems are just as imperfect as the humans that operate them. We should do what we can to fight injustice in any form, also within our social and juridical structures and systems.

If – in spite of all our striving – justice does not prevail at this moment, you can look at Jesus. He was convicted and executed unjustly: there has never been a more just man than he! He promised that one day, at the Last Judgement at the end of time, justice would take its course. But before we are there, we must promote justice everywhere, especially for the small, poor, and marginalised.

READ MORE

#TwGOD 4.3, 4.45; #OnlineSaints 2.24, 2.28.
Common good: CCC 1905-1917; CCCC 407-410; YOUCAT 327-328; DOCAT 87-88, 201.

PRAY

God, you invite us to learn from your mercy, which is rooted in divine justice. Help us to let love be our only guiding principle, also when applying a just penalty.

Reporting betrayal?

Jesus told us to correct our brother or sister who wrongs us, in private first of all, and if they do not listen then to repeat the denunciation in the presence of some others. If they still do not amend their ways, we are to report them to the community, in practice to its government *(Mt 18:15-17)*. Picking up the phone to report a crime to the authorities is therefore in line with Jesus' command and desire for people to be corrected so they can amend their ways. Note, however, that Jesus' indications were directed to the correction of the criminal, not to the retribution or vindication which is also part of our judicial system *(see Question 11)*. When people say that reporting someone to the police equals betrayal, they imply that the authorities will not give them a fair trial. Indeed, as Christians we cannot denounce someone to an unjust regime. In spite of all the flaws, most of our judicial systems have the intention of doing justice. But when this clearly is not the case, like when a dictator is known to make his enemies disappear, we have to refuse any collaboration.

QUOTE

Charity and justice

"The marginalised, the poor, the victims of all kinds of exploitation... are people who are experiencing in their own flesh the absence of peace and the terrible effects of injustice. Who can remain indifferent to their craving for a life rooted in justice and in genuine peace? It is everyone's responsibility to ensure that they achieve their desire: there can be no complete justice unless everyone shares in it equally... Justice makes whole, it does not destroy; it leads to reconciliation, not to revenge. Upon examination, at its deepest level it is rooted in love, which finds its most significant expression in mercy. Therefore justice, if separated from merciful love, becomes cold and cutting."

[Pope John Paul II, World Peace Day, 1 Jan. 1998, 1]

"Every society draws up its own system of justice. Charity goes beyond justice, because to love is to give, to offer what is 'mine' to the other; but it never lacks justice, which prompts us to give the other what is 'his', what is due to him by reason of his being or his acting. I cannot 'give' what is mine to the other, without first giving him what pertains to him in justice. If we love others with charity, then first of all we are just towards them. Not only is justice not extraneous to charity, not only is it not an alternative or parallel path to charity: justice is inseparable from charity."

[Pope Benedict XVI, Caritas in Veritate, 6]

SAINT

Divine justice

The archangel Michael is often depicted with a sword in one hand and scales in the other. The first is used to ward off evil, and the second to weigh our merits on Judgement Day. Thankfully the divine justice is better than ours and God's mercy always greater than we can imagine.

THINK

- Can the Bible change situations of injustice in your society? How?
- 'A just man has nothing to hide', so should the police have unlimited possibility to investigate people at will? Why (not)?

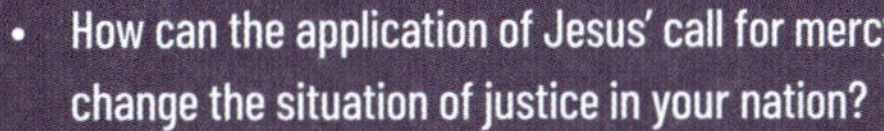

- How can the application of Jesus' call for mercy change the situation of justice in your nation?
- Have you ever reported a crime? Would you do it again? Why (not)?

ACT

How to deal with crime and punishment?

Modern judicial systems have been set up so that justice may take its course – not revenge. From a Christian perspective, many questions can and should be asked before administering possible punishment.

- The instinctive reaction of a community to a terrible crime in their midst may be to lynch the suspect. But is the suspect the culprit? Are there circumstances that diminish their guilt? Are they punishable, or was it self-defence, for example?
- 'Everyone tries to evade taxes, so if done on a small scale it is no problem.' 'A simple lie to get more insurance money is no real fraud.' Do you agree? Is it impossible to live a completely just life?
- A crime is a crime, right? But what if someone commits a crime in order to protect their partner in marriage or children who were kidnapped? Or what if a really poor person steals some food to feed their children? Are they guilty? Should they be punished?

These examples show that justice demands customisation and attention to the individuals concerned.

RECAP

Biblical justice is closely united with charity; our justice is not perfect and often lacks love. Wrongdoers should be punished with attention to their good and that of society.

Do we have a right to punish as Christians?

How could the saints say they were free while imprisoned?

Does the Bible condone modern slavery?

For God, love and justice are interconnected. Both are needed. A loving parent will sometimes punish a child for the child's own good. Until we arrive at our final destination in heaven, such reprimanding is sometimes necessary to correct and maintain the peace. In society, the prosecution and imposition of punishment is in the hands of the authorities. As long as they act in accordance with God's commandments – which unfortunately is not always the case – the civil authorities carry the sword of justice and are the "servant of God to execute wrath on the wrongdoer" *(Rom 13:4)*.

God's justice

In general, our judicial systems first of all seek punitive justice, punishing the culprit for their crime. The Bible does speak of the importance of punishment, but God's justice is mainly restorative: he searches to heal and repair. That is why Jesus took the punishment for our sins in our place, once and for all *(1 Jn 2:1-2)*. God is both just and merciful *(see Question 10)*. He always offers the culprit a new chance; if he must even seventy times seven times *(Mt 18:21-22)*. Catholics are opposed to the death penalty, as it contradicts God's love for life and does not allow for a new chance *(see #TwGOD 4.42)*.

More than punishment

A sentence at the conclusion of prosecution intends to achieve a number of things at the same time:

- Incapacitation, ensuring that the convicted person can not commit any further crimes. This has everything to do with the protection of society *(Jer 22:3)*.
- Deterrence, or discouragement of the culprit and others from committing a crime again. As such, it serves as prevention of further crime *(Ti 1:10-11)*.
- Retribution, or simply put 'getting even' is a form of vengeance, and as such unworthy of Christians. Did God not say "vengeance is mine"? *(Rom 12:19; see Question 10)*.

EXPLORE

A fist against human trafficking

The exploitation of people in any form is a flagrant disregard for human dignity. At first sight, certain Bible texts may seem to condone slavery *(Ex 21:20-21; Col 4:1)*, but read in context, Scripture condemns those who enslave others *(1 Tim 1:8-10)*. God intended each of us to be free *(Lk 4:18; Gal 5:1)*. Spiritually, this freedom can be experienced even when still enslaved *(1 Cor 7:21-24)*.

Sadly, there are still many forms of slavery today. This human trafficking takes various forms in which force, fraud or coercion are used to bring people into vicious circles of dependency. Forced labour of children and adults often is the result of becoming trapped in a system of dependency on their patrons through debt bondage, force, blackmail... Sex trafficking makes many children and adults victims of a pervert egoism that abuses others for personal pleasures. Other forms of modern slavery are forced marriages, child soldiers, domestic servitude, inherited slavery... This also happens in the so-called developed world.

The only possible Christian answer is to fight for a complete end to any form of human trafficking globally. We need to do this together as a society, but also as individuals. Whenever we buy products or services that are the result of slavery, we make ourselves into slaves of sin! "For freedom Christ has set us free. Stand firm, therefore, and do not submit again to a yoke of slavery" *(Gal 5:1)*.

- Punishment, a penalty imposed in response to criminal behaviour according to local law. It is payback time, without partiality *(Col 3:25)*. This is not the same as retribution, and more directed to a kind of restoration of what was done wrong.
- Reformation and rehabilitation are directed to helping those convicted to better their lives and prepare themselves for regaining a place in society *(Mk 2:17)*.

Christian prisons?

Prisons are an important way of keeping society safe from harmful individuals, and hopefully help them better their lives. For Christians, the punitive and especially the retributive part of a prison sentence is not the most glorious. These are necessary, but more important is the rehabilitation: how to help the person who stepped over the line once or repeatedly to regain that human dignity of the just? Conversely, sometimes the prison system tends to draw people further into a life of crime instead of helping them to reform and live an honest life. Add to this excessive violence of police forces, corrupt judges, and vicious wardens. Such great injustice should be corrected immediately.

READ MORE

#TwGOD 2.13, 4.11, 4.14, 4.42; #OnlineSaints 1.44, 2.27. *Punishment & Trafficking:* CCC 2266-2267 & 2414; CCCC 468-469; YOUCAT 435; DOCAT 228 & 151-153.

PRAY

Dear God, help me to walk always in truth and justice, and fight injustice and any restriction to human freedom. Inspire me to be free even if (unjustly) incarcerated.

Priests on trial

The Church has its own law book and judicial system with courts and possibilities of appeal. Church law, called canon law *(see #TwGOD 4.11)*, deals with the organisation of Catholic life. Many cases deal with typical internal Church problems like disobedience to superiors. However, if the misbehaviour is a crime, then the Church must report the suspect to the civil authorities, who will investigate and prosecute if there is a case.

A terrible example is the crime of sexual abuse. Next to the secular procedure, there usually there will also be a separate juridical procedure in the ecclesiastical court to establish how the culprit must be punished according to canon law.

As an independent state, the Vatican has the possibility of placing people in a detention cell while they are under investigation, and of imposing disciplinary action, including detention. As can be expected, there is no capital punishment in the Vatican state.

QUOTE

Prisons as an image of society

"Punishment cannot be reduced to mere retribution, much less take the form of social retaliation or a sort of institutional vengeance. Punishment and imprisonment have meaning if, while maintaining the demands of justice and discouraging crime, they serve the rehabilitation of the individual by offering those who have made a mistake an opportunity to reflect and to change their lives in order to be fully reintegrated into society." **[Pope John Paul II, Jubilee in prisons, 9 Jul. 2000, 6]**

"Prisons are an indication of the kind of society we live in. In many cases they are a sign of the silence and omissions which have led to a throwaway culture, a symptom of a culture that has stopped supporting life, of a society that has little by little abandoned its children... Reintegration or rehabilitation begins by creating a... system of social health that endeavours to promote a culture which acts and seeks to prevent those situations and pathways that end in damaging and impairing the social fabric." **[Pope Francis, Penitentiary of Ciudad Juárez, 17 Feb. 2016]**

SAINT

Oh Freedom

Titus Brandsma was unjustly incarcerated by the Nazis but kept his cool. In prison he wrote a prayer to Jesus, whom he called his special friend: "O, leave me here alone and still / With all around the cold and chill / Let no one ever come to me / With you the silence turns me free." He had an inner freedom and affection for Jesus which no one could take from him, not even by extreme force. The African-American spiritual 'Oh Freedom' speaks about a similar inner freedom: slaves do not necessarily consider themselves 'enslaved'. An unjust oppressor can chastise your body, but cannot change your heart or soul. There you are free to think and choose what you deem to be right and just.

THINK

- Is punishment a good way to teach people to change their ways? If a country applies the death penalty, will you still buy its products or visit it? Why (not)?
- Are fines effective as punishment or just a way to fill the pockets of the government? Why (not)?
- What kinds of possible slavery do you see in the world? What can Christians do?
- Do you think people leave prison as better people or better criminals? Why?

ACT

Is prison a good thing?

There are many questions with regard to the morality of imprisoning other people in reaction to their bad behaviour. Here are some thoughts.

- In most countries, a prisoner costs society yearly more than the minimum wage of a worker. 'They committed the crime, not I...Why should my taxes go to feeding a criminal in jail for many years if we can administer the death penalty and be done with it forever?' What would Jesus answer?
- We send people to prison to punish them, to take revenge, to protect society, to prevent, to re-educate... Which of these is the most important for you? And for God?
- An early release of prisoners can have a great positive effect. But there is also a danger of relapse. Should we still try to let inmates free when there are reasonable signs of improvement?
- But then there are places where the situation in prison is inhumane: too many inmates in a cell, corruption or abuse of power, gang control... What should the Christian answer be?

Maybe these few points can help you think about imprisonment in a new way.

RECAP

Crimes must be punished, not as revenge but to prevent crime and rehabilitate the offender. Slavery is a great wrong. In your heart you are free, even in prison.

What does the Bible say about discrimination?

What is social justice? Can I be self-sufficient? Does God want us to be weak?

Love, not the law, is the ultimate point of reference for Biblical justice. Jesus placed love for God and for our fellow human beings above anything else *(Mt 22:37-42)*. That should also be true for every form of our justice. Social justice strives for a better life for all. It is founded on the fundamental dignity of every human person *(see Basics)*. This requires a special attention to the rights of the weak, small, poor and minority groups. Social justice is related to all the themes in this book.

Common good

A football team cannot play well without each individual player giving their best. Conversely, the individual players cannot play a match all by themselves. We need each other as people, and cannot only seek our own interests *(Phil 2:4)*. Social justice demands that when we exercise our individual rights, we do so always with the good of the group in mind, the 'common good' *(see Basics)*.

The common good comprehends everything in social life that allows us to reach our fulfilment as a group and as individuals *(Gaudium et Spes, 26)*. The principle of solidarity tells us to share the goods and resources of society with everyone *(see Basics)*. In other words, that these are placed at the disposal of the common good. Although it may mean that I end up with less than I had individually, it also means that as a group we are much better off!

Interdependency

Complete self-sufficiency is an illusion: we always depend on God and fellow human beings in one way or another. We neither live nor die for ourselves *(Rom 14:7)*. A seller depends on buyers, a poor person on those who give, a service provider on patrons, an orphan on carers, an entertainer on the public, and a homeless person on those who offer shelter. When you share something with a person in need, you do not only help this individual, but also make a small contribution to a more just society, thus serving the common good. This dependency is also true between generations. Think of how parents care for their children and later children for their parents, but also of the quality of life, earth and society we leave for the next generation.

Defence of the weak

It would almost seem that God prefers us to be weak. Throughout the Bible he works with rather weak people as his chosen prophets *(Ex 4:10-16)*. And look at the Apostles with all their flaws! *(Mt 26:75)*. However, God does not want us to be weak: while he knows our weakness he tells us that he is not limited by it! *(Rom 8:3)*. Through our weakness, God can show his strength, thus in a way our weakness makes us strong! *(2 Cor 12:9-10)*. But this weakness can never be an excuse for not doing what we can to help people on the margins of society. Jesus first of all came to bring the good news of the Gospel to the outcast, the poor, the weary, the blind, the captives, the oppressed... *(Lk 4:18; Mt 11:28)*.

READ MORE

#TwGOD 1.3, 2.46-2.48, 3.50, 4.13 ; #OnlineSaints 2.24.
Social justice & Structures of sin: CCC 1928-1933, 2437-2441 & 1869; CCCC 411, 518 & 400; YOUCAT 329 & 320; DOCAT 108-111 & 191.

EXPLORE

No partiality or discrimination

We are all created by God in his own image and likeness *(Gen 1:26-27)*. So even if our outward appearance is different, how can you maintain that we have different value? Such discrimination is a great wrong *(Jn 7:24; Jas 2:2-4)*. As Saint Paul said, among the baptised "there is no longer Jew or Greek, there is no longer slave or free, there is no longer male and female; for all of you are one in Christ Jesus" *(Gal 3:28)*. This applies to every human being: we are all children of God. If we hate even one of our brothers or sisters in the world we are blind *(1 Jn 2:11)*.

People look at the outside, but God sees the heart *(1 Sam 16:7)*. Partiality and favouritism are against God's wishes *(1 Tim 5:21; Col 3:25)*, "for God shows no partiality" *(Rom 2:11)*. Saint James considered such behaviour a sin *(Jas 2:8-9)*, and wondered whether those who do this really believe in Jesus *(Jas 2:1-4)*. At the end of time we will just be a multitude from every nation, tribe, people and language, only distinguished by our choice for (or against) love *(Rev 7:9; 14:6)*. Every form of negative discrimination is wrong and sinful.

PRAY

Father of all, I abhor the fact that today people are victims of partiality and discrimination. Help me to give everything in the fight for social justice for all!

Structures of sin

All actions and structures that discriminate or marginalise certain members of society are contrary to the common good. This can be intentional or unintentional, but in the end is the result of selfish choices. It is a Christian duty to fight this evil, which takes many forms. For example, economic and social systems in which only those with money can advance themselves are in fact a hidden form of slavery: the poor cannot lend money because they have no collateral, thus they cannot invest or study, thus they remain poor... This happens also very close to home. For example, consumers of overly cheap goods and services are probably supporting structures of modern slavery and social oppression *(see Question 11)*.

QUOTE

The common good

"When interdependence becomes recognised... the correlative response... is solidarity. This then is not a feeling of vague compassion or shallow distress at the misfortunes of so many people, both near and far. On the contrary, it is a firm and persevering determination to commit oneself to the common good; that is to say to the good of all and of each individual, because we are all really responsible for all."

[Pope John Paul II, Sollicitudo Rei Socialis, 38]

"In the present condition of global society, where injustices abound and growing numbers of people are deprived of basic human rights and considered expendable, the principle of the common good immediately becomes, logically and inevitably, a summons to solidarity and a preferential option for the poorest of our brothers and sisters. This option... demands before all else an appreciation of the immense dignity of the poor in the light of our deepest convictions as believers."

[Pope Francis, Laudato si', 158]

SAINT

Smiling in the face of injustice

Martin de Porres is the patron saint of social justice. He was discriminated against because of his mixed race, his dark skin, his low descent... even in the monastery! Instead of growing a bitter man, he responded to insults with a smile, to servitude with love. His truly Christian answer helped many people change their minds about classic prejudices against race and descent.

THINK

- What forms of discrimination have you seen or experienced? What could you do?
- Are men better than women at certain tasks? Is that also true for people of a different racial background? Why (not)?
- What structures of sin are present in your society? What can you do as a Christian?
- How can 'social justice' help to create a better living environment for everyone?

ACT

Why is it not easy to help?

Defending the weak, helping the poor, standing up for those who are being discriminated against are important causes, but taking action can prove rather complicated in real life.

- Helping poor people is great, but do you not keep them in a state of dependency by simply giving them what they need? Is their human dignity not better served by offering them the opportunity to gain their lives? But then, how to avoid people feeling that they are in debt with you and becoming enslaved in a new way?
- Solidarity involves sacrifice *(see Question 1)*. But are there limits to your duty to stand up for others? For example, you may need your job to sustain your family, but then you discover that your boss has certain very uncharitable ideas and discriminates against people in his or her private life. Will you need to quit your job, or is their private life not your concern? And what if they start applying their discriminatory views also at work?
- You do not have much income. Then you discover that the cheap shirts you have been wearing for some time now have been made by child slaves. Will you stop wearing the shirts, or turn them into a monument in support of these child labourers? Will you rather dress shabbily instead of buying new cheap shirts from a similar source? And what if there is a dress code at work?

Standing up for your beliefs can have great consequences. It is up to you to choose in conscience what you consider the right and just thing to do. Do not forget to pray and to ask the Holy Spirit to help you discern!

RECAP

Social justice means a better life for all. Self-sufficiency is an illusion. All forms of discrimination are contrary to Jesus' desire for us to be free and flourish.

13

What are fundamental human rights?

Should everyone have the right to practise any religion? How far should I adapt to minorities?

Justice & Peace

Jesus wants us to live life to the full and to do so in all freedom *(Lk 4:18; Jn 10:10)*. Note, however, that absolute freedom does not exist here on earth. In heaven it does, but there we will have but one desire: to love God and our brothers and sisters. For all to live in freedom now, we need to give way to each other.

Music and silence

If I like loud music and you like silence, we both will have to accept some limits to our freedom as long as we are living in hearing distance of each other. On the streets we accept that traffic rules limit our freedom for the safety of all. The state can and should impose certain limits to freedom *(see Question 23)*. But always for the good of individuals or the community, and with respect for fundamental human rights. These human rights apply to every human being, regardless of race, sex, religion, or lifestyle, for example. They include the right to life, work, freedom from slavery, freedom of opinion...

Human rights

Much of the Universal Declaration of Human Rights of the United Nations is a great reflection of God's Commandments *(Ex 20:2-17; see #TwGOD 4.9)*. This does not mean that the United Nations is Christian. It merely shows how our human way of being and relating corresponds profoundly with the biblical view. If we believe that God created every human person, that should not come as a surprise. Even when they do not confess the Christian faith, every human being is a child of the same Father in heaven. As Christians, we have to love them as our brothers and sisters, and respect their freedom to choose for love (or against it). Human rights help us to do so.

EXPLORE

Destroying statues?

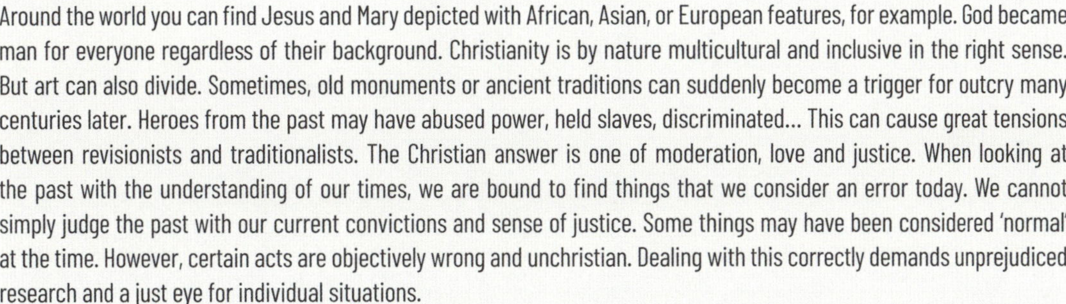

Around the world you can find Jesus and Mary depicted with African, Asian, or European features, for example. God became man for everyone regardless of their background. Christianity is by nature multicultural and inclusive in the right sense. But art can also divide. Sometimes, old monuments or ancient traditions can suddenly become a trigger for outcry many centuries later. Heroes from the past may have abused power, held slaves, discriminated... This can cause great tensions between revisionists and traditionalists. The Christian answer is one of moderation, love and justice. When looking at the past with the understanding of our times, we are bound to find things that we consider an error today. We cannot simply judge the past with our current convictions and sense of justice. Some things may have been considered 'normal' at the time. However, certain acts are objectively wrong and unchristian. Dealing with this correctly demands unprejudiced research and a just eye for individual situations.

Society may have praised for generations a family which helped thousands of poor orphans. And then we discover that like their neighbours they had many slaves... Their good work does not change the fact that slavery is a great wrong. But we can still recognise a particularly benevolent master who was good to their slaves, while condemning slavery, for example. We cannot erase what has happened, and have to find the best way to live with the past today. Will you close that very useful tunnel which was dug by slaves because of how it was made, or can you better honour their work and suffering by making good use of it? It may be effective to keep monuments as a warning against injustice. But it may also be that justice is better served by changing a tradition – even if you believe it is not wrong – because other people in society take offence. Whatever you decide, let love have the last word.

Religious freedom

One of the fundamental human rights is religious freedom *(1 Pt 2:16)*. Only when you are truly free can you choose to love God in response to his great love. I cannot decide for you what your religion will be. I can hope and pray that you will see how much happier you will be if you become a Christian, but you should be free to choose differently. I too may expect to be free in my religious choices. Yes, we can and should share the joyful message of the Gospel with everyone *(Mt 28:19; see Question 26)*. But we should also welcome them as they are and give them the freedom to exercise their religion just as we want to be free to exercise ours.

READ MORE

#TwGOD 1.8, 2.26, 4.45;
#OnlineSaints 1.15, 1.29.
Other religions: CCC 839-848; CCCC 169-171; YOUCAT 135136; DOCAT 327-328.

PRAY

God of love and freedom, help me to respect the freedom of every human being while trying to live in love with everyone.

Limits and rights

Fundamental rights should be respected, but there are limits. For example, if a religious group intends to bring human sacrifices to their gods it needs to be stopped. Here the fundamental right of freedom of religion is clashing with the fundamental right to life. But it is not always true that minorities have to adapt in everything to a predominant religion: they too have rights.

QUOTE

Human rights

"The Universal Declaration of Human Rights... was the outcome of a convergence of different religious and cultural traditions, all of them motivated by the common desire to place the human person at the heart of institutions, laws and the workings of society, and to consider the human person essential for the world of culture, religion and science... They are based on the natural law inscribed on human hearts and present in different cultures and civilizations... This great variety of viewpoints must not be allowed to obscure the fact that not only rights are universal, but so too is the human person, the subject of those rights." **[Pope Benedict XVI, to the General Assembly of the UN, 18 April 2008]**

"The Universal Declaration of Human Rights... favours what the Church's social doctrine calls integral human development... The interpretation of some rights has progressively changed... debatable notions of human rights have been advanced that are at odds with the culture of many countries; the latter feel that they are not respected in their social and cultural traditions, and instead neglected with regard to the real needs they have to face... At the same time, it should be recalled that the traditions of individual peoples cannot be invoked as a pretext for disregarding the due respect for the fundamental rights proclaimed by the Universal Declaration of Human Rights."

[Pope Francis, To the diplomatic corps, 8 Jan. 2018]

SAINT

Persecution of Christians

Both Marije Tuci and Jerzy Popiełuszko were persecuted because of their faith by communists who tried to enforce a form of atheism. Peacefully they resisted the unjust suppression by standing up for their religious freedom. Thus they supported the people around them in their faith. Ironically, their persecution and violent death further inspired the faithful. Sadly, also today many Christians are persecuted because of their faith.

THINK

- Is it truly possible to give the same fundamental rights to every person in the world? How?
- Should there be limits to the freedom of speech? Why (not)?
- 'Religion and human rights do not mix.' Do you agree? Why (not)?
- Have you ever been silenced from expressing your religion? Or felt like you wanted to silence others? How was that?

ACT

How does religious freedom work in practice?

The fundamental right of religious freedom can place people before complicated decisions. How can you ensure that you respect the freedom of others and are free to exercise your freedom at the same time? How far should you adapt?

- Take a country that is predominantly Christian. Should an atheist girl wear the skirts that her strict Christian employers request instead of her jeans? Should a Christian woman give in to the desire of her Muslim employers to cover her head? Should a Muslim be free to wear a hijab, even when working for Christian employers? Should emergency aid workers respect the wish of a patient to be touched only by a man or a woman, even if this is considered discriminatory and means risking the patient's life?
- Now take a country that is predominantly Muslim. Should a Christian woman start wearing a headscarf in public for that is the norm? Should a Jew be obliged to avoid alcohol because strict Muslims do not drink? Should an atheist woman take a submissive attitude to her husband in public?
- Ladies covering their head in a mosque and gentlemen donning a kippah in the synagogue or taking off their cap in a church do not make concessions to the deity that is worshipped there, but show respect for the humans who worship there. But how far should your respect for other religions go? Will you take off the little crucifix around your neck if that may offend others? Should everyone refrain from any religious symbols to keep the peace in society? Or should they accept these as being part of the way individuals are?

The answers to these questions partly depend on circumstances. They result from a clash of fundamental rights. The right of the individual to exercise their religion is very fundamental. But the highest ruling principle remains love!

RECAP

Every human person has the right to life, religion, freedom, work... Absolute freedom does not exist: we need to adapt our ways to guarantee each other's freedom.

Is it at all possible to have peace everywhere?

Can I contribute? How should we react to genocide, dictatorship, annexation or arms trade?

True peace is intrinsically related to justice and a fair sharing of wealth, resources and opportunities *(see Question 1)*. "Peace is not merely the absence of war", the bishops of the world wrote *(Gaudium et Spes, 78)*. Peace is more than just a balance of power between enemies: it is an enterprise of justice that involves all humanity. Humanly it may seem impossible that one day there will be peace in all the world. But the God of peace wants to be with us at this moment *(Rom 15:33)*. Jesus was announced as the Prince of Peace *(Isa 9:6)*. He tells us also now: "Peace I leave with you; my peace I give to you" *(Jn 14:27)*. As Christians we are to do what we can to bring about lasting peace in this world.

Peace in our lives

Our first contribution to peace in the world is by bringing peace into every aspect of our own lives *(see Act)*. That in itself is quite an enterprise, for human beings carry so much anger, hatred and violence in themselves. But the saints show how it is possible to let these negative emotions flow away and let them be replaced by the peace that Jesus wants to give *(see Saint)*. Pray regularly, and let yourself be transformed slowly by God's peace. You may have experienced a sense of peace in a church or a monastery, an enclosed garden or on the open sea. Also certain people can help you find inner peace, just by being present. With the grace of God you too can be such a beacon of peace: "Blessed are the peacemakers, for they will be called children of God" *(Mt 5:9)*.

Mutual trust

There are many ways in which peace can be fostered. A nation can provide neutral ground and promote moderation in diplomatic negotiations between parties in conflict. But also at the grassroot level it is possible to contribute to peace. This can be done in schools, teaching the Christian principles of love, even for the enemy. Or by bringing ordinary people from both sides together for an experience of brotherhood. People, not ideas should be the most important in searching for a solution. Often, conflicts continue and harden because of misunderstanding and mistrust. Fostering mutual trust is a very important step towards lasting peace. As Pope John XXIII said: "The world will never be the dwelling place of peace, till peace has found a home in the heart of each and every man, till every man preserves in himself the order ordained by God to be preserved" *(Pacem in terris, 165)*.

Mediation or intervention?

Surely, we should send in the army when a people is suffering under a dictator, genocide, or occupation? Or should nations limit their international interventions to mediation? This is a very complicated question to answer in general, just as it is very difficult to answer it in specific situations. It is true that the defence of the weak and marginalised is a Christian duty *(see Question 1)*. It is also true that we can use a just amount of armed resistance to keep them from harm *(see #TwGOD 4.43)*. The violence used must always be in proportion to the force of the attack, and minimise human injury as much as possible.

There is a Christian concept of 'just war', which states that in certain circumstances war can be the only means to obtain peace – after all other attempts of establishing peace have been tried *(see #TwGOD 4.44)*. But whatever its cause, war is always a defeat of humanity! War can never be truly just, which is why we rather speak of 'just peace'. It is our Christian duty to do what we can to bring this just peace about! Every army has as its ultimate goal its own redundancy at the moment the world will have found peace *(see #TwGOD M.1)*.

EXPLORE

Arms trade?

What if my country supports one of the parties in an armed conflict, saying it strives for peace, but at the same time sells arms to the other party? Unfortunately this happens more often than we think. The production, selling, and possession of weapons is unlike other trade, and connected to great ethical and social questions. The more destructive these arms are, the worse the moral responsibility of all involved. Nuclear arms and cluster bombs, for example, are so destructive that their use and even their possession cannot be morally admissible *(see Quote)*.

READ MORE

#TwGOD 4.42-4.44; #OnlineSaints 1.11, 2.26-2.27.
Peace: CCC 2263-2265, 2304-2317; CCCC 467, 481-486; YOUCAT 380, 395-399; DOCAT 67-68, 270-300.

PRAY

God of peace, I thank you for giving us Jesus, the Prince of Peace. Help me to live in peace with all people and spread peace around me.

Reconciliation

Reconciliation is a very important step in bringing about peace. This is where the words of the Our Father compel us concretely: "Forgive us our trespasses as we forgive those who have trespassed against us" *(Mt 6:12)*. This is easy to say, but demands an act of will to become reality. God reconciled us to himself through Jesus. And he has given us the task of bringing about reconciliation ourselves *(2 Cor 5:18)*. Those who strive for reconciliation between parties are doing God's work: "Blessed are the peacemakers" *(Mt 5:9)*.

QUOTE

Peace is possible

"True and lasting peace among nations cannot consist in the possession of an equal supply of armaments but only in mutual trust. And we are confident that this can be achieved."

[Pope John XXIII, Pacem in Terris, 113]

"The arms race wastes precious resources that could be better used to benefit the integral development of peoples and to protect the natural environment. In a world where millions of children and families live in inhumane conditions, the money that is squandered and the fortunes made through the manufacture, upgrading, maintenance and sale of ever more destructive weapons, are an affront crying out to heaven. A world of peace, free from nuclear weapons, is the aspiration of millions of men and women everywhere."

[Pope Francis, On nuclear weapons, 24 Nov. 2019

"Peace is not essentially about structures but about people. Certain structures and mechanisms of peace - juridical, political, economic - are of course necessary and do exist, but they have been derived from nothing other than the accumulated wisdom and experience of innumerable gestures of peace made by men and women throughout history who have kept hope and have not given in to discouragement. Gestures of peace spring from the lives of people who foster peace first of all in their own hearts... Religion has a vital role in fostering gestures of peace and in consolidating conditions for peace."

[Pope John Paul II, World Peace Day, 1 Jan. 2003, 9]

SAINT

A stance for peace

Catherine of Siena was a remarkable woman. In everything she did and said she gave evidence of a great personal faith. She conversed with the poor and popes alike. As an ambassador of the republic of Florence she strove for peace. She told the pope bluntly that he should no longer hide himself in France, but return to Rome. And he did! A few years later Florence and Rome signed a peace treaty. Catherine died young, but has a lasting influence through her example and prayer.

THINK

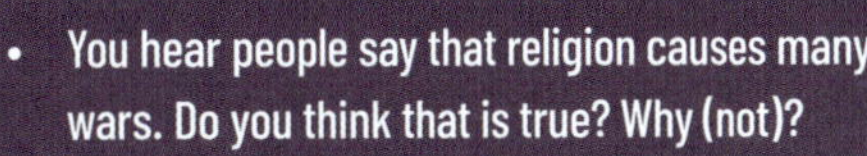

- If in church you hear 'Peace be with you', what kind of peace is intended?
- What is your experience with reconciliation? How would you help others to be reconciled?
- You hear people say that religion causes many wars. Do you think that is true? Why (not)?
- What can you do personally to promote peace?

ACT

In what sense does world peace start at home?

When speaking about world peace, there is so much that you cannot do. But try to see how much you can do!

- 'I feel guilty living in freedom while others suffer violence and war.' If that is how you feel, your heart is in the right place. Being close to those who suffer in your heart and prayer is the beginning of every action. What small actions could you take to spread peace around you?
- It is very helpful to strive for inner peace. You can create peaceful moments in your day that help you face events with a calm attitude. Thus you can bring peace to yourself and others.
- When you pray, you open yourself to the source of all peace, God. This is bound to have an influence on your life. And praying for others is a great way of being close to people in war zones, for example. Do you pray for peace sometimes?
- You can become a diplomat, or choose to join the armed forces of your country. You can also choose to be a conscientious objector. Whatever your choice is, let it come from deep inside you, and take the decision together with God. Would you like to contribute to peace in this way?

If you let yourself be led by the peaceful inspiration of Jesus, you too can make a real contribution to lasting world peace. If we all do that, the world will truly become a different place!

RECAP

World peace is possible with the help of God! Your first contribution should be to bring peace in your life. And we should also do what we can to prevent injustice as a society.

'Love your enemies', can it be done?

Are there parallels between Catholicism and the military?
How can I choose between serving myself or the common good?

Justice & Peace

"Love your enemies, do good to those who hate you, bless those who curse you, pray for those who mistreat you" *(Lk 6:27-28)*. These may well be among the most controversial words of Jesus. Even today we are struggling greatly to apply them. The theory is beautiful, but how can you feel love for this criminal who hurt you or those dear to you, that gossiping person who spread lies about you, or the terrorist trying to bomb you? How could Jesus have given us such an impossible commandment?

Saints

No, this is not about turning your enemies into your friends. It is indeed about feeling love for those who proabably will remain your enemies. God is love *(1 Jn 4:8)*. As he created us out of love, love is the foundation of all our existence. You will know how much better you feel when you love someone than when you hate them. Loving your enemies is going to help you too. Still, love does not always come more easily than hatred.

Human faces

So, how can you go about this? First of all, pray, for you cannot do this alone. Trying to see the enemy as persons with faces, fears, worries, and desires makes them more human and possibly more likeable. Also, try to see the situation from their perspective, ready to give up some of your own convictions. Furthermore, do not follow the bad example of others. Unfortunately, even in the Church some people have their harsh judgement ready at all times. Forgiving your enemy and praying for them are important steps towards loving them *(Mk 11:25; Mat 5:44)*.

Yes, we can!

It is possible to learn to love your enemy. Jesus prayed with love for those who had just crucified him *(Lk 23:34)*. If you try honestly, and ask God to help you with his grace, you too can do this. Imagine what would happen if all Jesus' followers actually lived this commandment. It would be an enormous step forward out of the mess we created on this earth!

EXPLORE

Catholics & the military

The Vatican has its own army of Swiss Guards, with more colourful uniforms than most armed forces, and less weaponry than any *(see #TwGOD 2.6)*. There are some interesting parallels between service in the military and service in the Church. Think of the concept of fraternity or comradery, with people being part of a group in which everyone contributes a little piece to a much larger whole. Think also of the clear moral standards, traditions, rituals, uniforms, the hierarchy...

Another parallel is in the serious dedication to a common goal. Where clerks in a government office can withdraw from their job when it threatens to becomes dangerous, soldiers cannot do so. They have promised to serve a greater good, if need be even by endangering their own life. Christians too are called to be ready to lay down their lives, rather than give in to the enemy of God, who tries to turn us away from all that is good, beautiful, and true *(1 Pt 5:8)*.

When someone joins the military, it will hopefully be out of an altruistic desire of service to the common good. Obviously also attractions like a clear position, educational possibilities, fixed income, and adventure will play a role. Similarly, people will ask 'what's in it for me?' when they join the Church. A desire to dedicate themselves to Jesus more than to themselves will need to be present. But most of us are still far away from a fully selfless lifestyle in which we can say "it is no longer I who live, but it is Christ who lives in me" *(Gal 2:20)*.

Obviously, there are also differences. You may object that the Church stands for peace, and the military for war. In fact, that is not true, for the ultimate aim of the military is its own redundancy on the day that peace will have been achieved everywhere. The military is temporary, and has a role only in this world. The Church is of supernatural origin, founded by God to lead us to him in heaven. Where the military serves the people of a given country, all faithful together form the Church, and all are called to join in her mission.

READ MORE

#TwGOD 4.3, 4.44; #OnlineSaints 1.2, 1.43.
Love for enemies: CCC 2608, 2646, 2844;
CCCC 544, 554, 595; YOUCAT 34, 487.

PRAY

God of all, help me see how loving my enemies and serving the common good will contribute to my personal happiness, for this means loving and serving you.

Institutional balance

The democratic model is based on a balance between separate powers. The legislative power passes the laws, the executive power implements them, and the judicial power ensures that the laws are complied with properly. Each of these is essential in keeping the others in check so that the common good is served and the system not abused. But there is more. Journalists, for example, play an important role in controlling the government and denouncing abuse.

The Church has an essential role here too, usually separate from the state *(see Question 22)*. The Church's message is important for the common good of society, hence her great desire to bring the peace and love of Christ to everyone. The police and military form the strong hand of the executive power. Their main task is to promote peace. This is considered so essential for the common good of all people, that peace is also 'exported' during missions abroad. Similarly, the Church's missionaries want to 'export' and promote God's love wherever people are *(Mk 16:15)*.

QUOTE

Combat

"The worship of God is contrary to the culture of hatred. And the culture of hatred is fought by combatting the cult of complaint. How many times do we complain about the things that we lack, about the things that go wrong! Jesus knows about all the things that don't work. He knows that there is always going to be someone who dislikes us. Or someone who makes our life miserable. All he asks us to do is pray and love. This is the revolution of Jesus, the greatest revolution in history: from hating our enemy to loving our enemy; from the cult of complaint to the culture of gift. If we belong to Jesus, this is the road we are called to take! There is no other."

[Pope Francis, Homily in Bari, 23 Feb. 2020]

SAINT

Serving God and country

Henry Dormer came from a long family tradition of military service to England. He was gazetted as an ensign in the 60th Regiment (King's Own Royal Rifles) and in 1866 he was sent to London, Canada. His fellow officers soon discovered Henry's great devotion to God. He often took care of poor, sick, and elderly people, and spoke openly about his faith. He was 21 years old when he died of typhoid fever, and was buried with military honours.

THINK

- How would you define the 'common good' in your own words? How can you serve it?
- Did you ever think about joining military or public service? Is that important?
- Is it reasonable to invest in weapons for military peace-keeping missions when people are starving? Why (not)?
- Should Christians be absolute pacifists? Why (not)?

ACT

Serving the common good?

People can never be considered solely in themselves, but always in relationship with others *(Rom 14:7)*. By serving the 'common good' of society you serve both others and yourself, for you are part of that society. Thus you can wonder why so many people choose to serve themselves above all...

- If you come from a culture where the collective is more important than the individual, or even when you were raised in a large family, you may be used to setting aside some of your own desires for the good of the group.
- Conversely, in an individualistic society, like much of the Western world, it will be much more difficult to get people to subject themselves to the needs of the group, for they are used to deciding for themselves first.
- The latter kind of society will have less appreciation than the former for the sacrifices of veterans who fought for the common good, or emergency aid workers, for example.
- Especially in the Western world, many people are happy in their private life, but can be quite negative about the public life in their societies. Obviously this makes the promotion of the common good more difficult.
- For Jesus there is no clear distinction between serving the good of others or yourself: "In everything do to others as you would have them do to you" *(Mt 7:12)*.

In conclusion, the service to the common good will bring happiness to both individuals and the group, but it takes a personal conversion to see this.

RECAP

With faith, loving your enemies is possible. Catholics and the military are dedicated to serving the common good. As you are relationship in yourself, the common good is your good too.

YOUR
NEIGHBOUR
IS GOD

ECONOMY & WORK

How can my job serve God?

Do I have a right to work? Is unemployment unchristian? What if I have to choose between church and work?

Economy & Work

Work, and especially manual labour, plays an important role in Jesus' teaching *(Mt 13:3-8; Jn 6:27)*. God ordered the first people to 'work the earth' *(Gen 2:15)*. This includes any useful activity, also at home or as a volunteer. Jesus worked as a carpenter *(Mk 6:3)*. Work is a way to realise our human dignity and to serve God so that we can strive for holiness. Becoming holy (sanctification) is the highest aim of our lives *(1 Thess 4:3)*. Through our work we are preparing for life in eternity with God.

Work as a vocation

In an economic sense, the right to work in return for fair wages is a fundamental right. This includes the right to private property, join a union, employ economic initiative... At the same time, workers are to do a good job, be diligent and honest, work for the good of all... Every job can be considered a calling, because you are 'working the earth' as God commanded *(Gen 2:15)*. God has a plan for each of us *(see #TwGOD 4.1)*. Because he created you, you can find the answer to your vocation deep inside yourself.

Working conditions

The abuse of workers in the industrial revolution prompted a papal response. A handful of business owners became immensely rich. But payments were low and working conditions often very bad. Masses of workers toiled daily for 12 or 14 hours in huge factories. Think of semi-dark, dirty industrial halls with very noisy machines oozing toxic fumes and liquids. Or think of miners using such machines deep under the ground. Such circumstances are in opposition to human dignity. Workers were not organised and at the mercy of their employers. Some honourable industry bosses tried to be good employers, but even in their factories working conditions were extremely bad compared to today's standards. There was no insurance, no one to speak up for the workers. An accident resulting in invalidity meant poverty for the rest of your life.

EXPLORE

Work or church?

Sometimes you may not be able to go to church because you have to work. God knows you need your job to live, and will not be angry if for reasons beyond your control you cannot attend church. However, not only do you have a right to work, but also a right to freely exercise your religion. There is a great difference between a roster that sees every employee work on Sundays and feast days occasionally, and a systematic violation of your rights. What you can do yourself on a 'working Sunday' is to take a short moment of quiet to pray and to be thankful to God. And try to go to church on Saturday evening or another day of the week.

God rested after the creation of the world *(Gen 2:2-3)* and ordered us to take weekly rests too *(Deut 5:14)*. From the beginning of Christianity, the 'first day of the week' was especially dedicated to worship *(Acts 20:7)*. In Christian countries, Sundays often are collective days of rest on which most commercial businesses and factories are closed. If you read the Old Testament, it would seem that no-one can do any work on a Sunday – our equivalent of the Jewish sabbath (celebrated on Saturday). While upholding this principle in general, Jesus explained that we do not live for our weekly rest, but it is there for our good *(Mk 2:27)*. Some people will have to work on Sundays, but letting go entirely of the Sunday rest is not a good idea for our societies.

Revolutionary change

In response to this situation, Pope Leo XIII wrote an open letter entitled *Rerum Novarum*, 'of revolutionary change'. He laid down several principles with regard to work that are true today as they were then. He called for better working conditions and payment. He also affirmed the right to form labour unions. He rejected both socialism and unlimited capitalism: private property is a right, but the free market must be regulated so that everyone is justly served *(see Question 17)*. This was the first time a pope had spoken so clearly about this theme, but the ideas were not new of course. The Bible condemns people who become rich by abusing their workers *(Jas 5:4-5)*, treating them unjustly *(Jer 22:13)*, or withholding wages *(Deut 24:14)*. Employers can pay workers different wages, as long as each receives a just pay *(Mt 20:1-16)*.

READ MORE

#TwGOD 4.1-4.6, 4.9; #OnlineSaints 1.8-1.10, 1.12-1.14.
Vocation of laity & Work: CCC 897-913 & 2426-2431;
CCCC 188-191 & 513-514; YOUCAT 139 & 444; DOCAT 134-140.

PRAY

Dear God, I am grateful that through my work I can realise my vocation. Help me to promote good working conditions and just wages for all.

Common good

Even if not everyone manages to get their dream job, all work contributes to the common good *(see Basics)*. There is no need to feel ashamed or greedy if you receive a just pay for your work. That said, if you have a good salary, you can decide to share part of it with your brothers and sisters who have less. Or even offer them a job so they can earn their living in a dignified way!

QUOTE

Work for the poor

"Some opportune remedy must be found quickly for the misery and wretchedness pressing so unjustly on the majority of the working class: for the ancient workingmen's guilds were abolished in the last century, and no other protective organization took their place... Working men have been surrendered, isolated and helpless, to the hardheartedness of employers and the greed of unchecked competition."

[Pope Leo XIII, Rerum Novarum, 3]

"We were created with a vocation to work... Work is a necessity, part of the meaning of life on this earth, a path to growth, human development and personal fulfilment. Helping the poor financially must always be a provisional solution in the face of pressing needs. The broader objective should always be to allow them a dignified life through work."

[Pope Francis, Laudato si', 128]

SAINT

Working saints

Saint Joseph the carpenter *(Mt 13:55)* shows how our work can bring us closer to God: it sanctifies us. Pope Pius XII instituted the celebration of 'Saint Joseph the worker' on 1 May in response to the Socialist and Communist 'May Day'. As Saint John Paul II said: "At the workbench where he plied his trade together with Jesus, Joseph brought human work closer to the mystery of the Redemption" *(Redemptoris Custos, 22)*. *Ora et labora*, Saint Benedict said, pray and work *(see Question 7)*. That is a great lead for you too in your daily life!

THINK

- Are you a hard worker? Is it wrong to be a workaholic? Why (not)?
- What qualities should a Christian boss have? And a Christian employee?
- Is it more important to like your job or to receive a just payment?
- People complain a lot about work. How can it be made more attractive?

ACT

Why should my salary pay for the unemployed?

It is very sad when people are unemployed through no fault of their own. Many people want to work, but there may not be enough work for each of them. A few thoughts.

- The sad reality of unemployment is not new: also in Jesus' time people hung around without finding a job for the day *(Mt 20:1-16)*. The Bible tells us how important it is to take care of these unemployed. Thus a landowner ordered his harvesters to leave some of the grain in the field for the poor to pick up *(Ruth 2:15-16)*.
- It is a Christian duty of people who have work to financially support those who do not. This is an important short-term answer. But receiving payment without working for it if you can is contrary to human dignity *(2 Thess 3:10)*. It is very important to stimulate the creation of jobs. Do you have ideas on how this can be done?
- 'The unemployed are profiteers who refuse to work', you may hear. Every form of fraud should be combated, of course. But so must every form of injustice, including the lack of work. Could our Christian duty of solidarity be so important that we can even risk to be cheated sometimes?
- Sometimes, a vicious circle needs to be broken: someone without a job will get tired of hanging around, becomes depressed, has no energy to search for a job... If you try to see things from the side of the unemployed, you will hopefully better understand the need for solidarity, both in the form of financial support and the creation of jobs. Do you think these should be useful jobs?

Solidarity is a key Christian principle that will help you often when faced with complex questions.

RECAP

Everyone has a right to work. As a Christian, your work is part of your vocation and helps your sanctification. Sunday rest is important, but so are certain jobs.

Does the Church support workers or employers?

Is the right to property Christian? Can I move work to 'cheap countries'? Does the Church discriminate against women?

"The labourer deserves to be paid", Jesus said *(Lk 10:7)*. Not only do we have a right to work *(see Question 16)* but also to receive a just pay for the work done. Admittedly, money is only a temporary reward, as we strive for a higher reward in heaven. Until we are there, our wages should allow us at least to pay for the minimal necessities of life. Some claim that a legal minimum wage reduces competition and, in the end, causes more unemployment. For others, a minimum wage helps to ensure the wellbeing of all. The latter is in line with the dignity of the worker and the principle of solidarity *(see Basics)*.

Does the Church take sides?

In the Christian view, workers and employers need each other as they work towards their sanctification *(see Question 16)*. Employees will work with dedication for the goal of their employers, and can expect a just treatment and payment in return. Employers will respond by running their businesses well, with care for those who work for them. There is nothing wrong with making a profit, for without it an employer cannot offer any work!

Both employees and employers are important to the Church, which supports especially those who are marginalised in any way. She defends employees against oppression and extortion, but also employers that face impossible demands from their employees *(see Quote)*. Employees may wonder what exactly their workers unions achieve and employers may consider them a nuisance, but the principal intention of labour unions is very Christian.

Cheap labour?

At times the need for profit and the care for employees may seem to be at odds: how can you compete in a market where extremely cheap products from abroad are available? It seems logical to consider moving production to a low-income country, where wages are more competitive with regard to the international market prices. The salaries would be just in comparison

EXPLORE

Does the Church discriminate?

At the creation God intended humankind as men or as women *(Gen 1:27)*. They have absolute equal value and should be treated accordingly *(see #TwGOD 2.16)*. Any unjust discrimination, like giving a lower salary to a woman than to a man for the same work, is greatly wrong. But does the Church not discriminate too when only men can become priests? Well, that depends on your viewpoint. For starters, priesthood is but one of the many vocations in the Church. Every vocation is infinitely important. In fact, in most Church roles there are more women than men! But we cannot do everything we want: a man cannot become a nun, nor can he by nature carry a child in his womb. Men and women can be good at different tasks while being completely equal in value. A vocation is given to you by God and cannot be grasped for yourself.

The popes concluded from extensive theological research that God wants only males as priests *(see #TwGOD 3.41)*. But this does not mean in any way an exclusion of women! Rather, it is the consequence of the recognition of the specific contribution each of the sexes are called to give. Jesus had many female followers, and first showed himself to a woman after his resurrection *(see Saint)*. However, we cannot claim that everything is done well today. It is true that more women should be involved in the government of the Church, for example. Thankfully, there is a growing attention, but much still needs to be done *(see #OnlineSaints 1.47-1.48)*.

to the local economic situation there. On the other hand, this takes away work from one's own country, where people need it too. And then there is the damage to the environment caused by long distance transportation...

Shared responsibility

There are many factors to be taken into account here. Not profit but people should be the determining factor. Work, opportunities and resources should be shared as fairly as possible. We are to do so each within our own sphere of influence first. If an employer has to choose between leaving people unemployed at home or far away, it seems logical that he gives precedence to those that are already in his care if that is a feasible option. Consumers also play a role: do you really like those dirt-cheap articles you just bought, when you think of the bad working conditions that make such a low price possible? *(see Question 11)*.

READ MORE

#TwGOD 2.45, 4.45, 2.16;
#OnlineSaints 1.4-1.5, 1.48-1.49.
Workers rights: CCC 2433-2436; CCCC 515, 517;
YOUCAT 445; DOCAT 142-150, 154-157.

PRAY

God, you created us for work. Help me support dignified working conditions, equal opportunities, just remuneration, and collaboration between workers and employers.

Private property

If you have a right to payment, you must also have a right to keep and use it as you deem proper. This is part of the motivation to work at all! The first Christians sold all their possessions and had everything in common *(Acts 2:44-45)*. In monastic life this is still the case. But those of us 'in the world' have a right to private property *(see Quote)*. We need to provide for ourselves and our families, also for the future, so keeping a just reserve of savings is a sensible thing to do. The Bible encourages such providing as good stewardship *(Prov 24:27; Lk 14:28)*. Saint Paul tells us to save regularly, if only to pay community taxes: "On the first day of every week, each of you is to put aside and save whatever extra you earn" *(1 Cor 16:2)*. At the same time, Jesus warned against the blind accumulation of wealth here on earth: we cannot take it with us to heaven! *(Lk 12:15-21)*.

QUOTE

Right to property and union

"The socialists, working on the poor man's envy of the rich, are striving to do away with private property, and contend that individual possessions should become the common property of all, to be administered by the state or by municipal bodies... They would rob the lawful possessor, distort the functions of the state, and create utter confusion in the community. It is surely undeniable that, when a man engages in remunerative labour, the impelling reason and motive of his work is to obtain property, and thereafter to hold it as his very own."

[Pope Leo XIII, Rerum Novarum, 4-5]

"The important role of union organisations must be admitted... Their activity, however, is not without its difficulties. Here and there the temptation can arise of profiting from a position of force to impose, particularly by strikes - the right to which as a final means of defence remains certainly recognised - conditions which are too burdensome for the overall economy and for the social body, or to desire to obtain in this way demands of a directly political nature."

[Pope Paul VI, Octogesima Adveniens, 14]

SAINT

Witness of Jesus' love

Mary Magdalene was among the closest followers of Jesus. The Bible records her as the first person to see Jesus after his resurrection. She, not a male Apostle, received the first mission to announce how he had defeated death. Mary is celebrated as an Apostle of the faith by the Church, for thanks to her testimony we know about what happened at the empty tomb of Jesus at Easter.

THINK

- What jobs in society are underpaid? Which ones are overpaid? Is this difference fair?
- Should desk jobs be paid better than manual labour? Why (not)?
- What can Christians do to promote the equal treatment of every human being?
- 'Minimum wages force investors to move elsewhere.' Do you agree?

ACT

A maximum wage?

It seems unfair that an educated and skilled carpenter earns less than an educated and skilled surgeon. Neither will probably have to live on a minimum wage, but the differences are striking.

- Some say this difference can be explained because of the longer study and greater investment for some professions. If the payment were not above average, would people make the effort? We need both surgeons and carpenters. But if they both work similar hours, shouldn't they be paid similar wages?
- A distinction in payment for different work is acceptable, as long as everyone is assured a minimum income and the principle of solidarity is applied *(Mt 20:1-16)*. The free market is important for the economy to flourish, which is good for all in society. But can wages become excessively high? Do you think there should be something like a maximum wage?
- People are paid more if their work is in demand, dangerous, requires longer education or more responsibility. But how you define 'dangerous' or 'more responsibility'? And should there be extra pay also for jobs that are tedious or dirty, for example?

The market cannot always regulate itself and government invention may be needed to assure justice and the wellbeing of all.

RECAP

Our human dignity is reflected in worker's rights. The Church supports workers and employers in their search for sanctification through work. She fights unjust discrimination.

Is there a Christian business model?

What if my boss tells me to act unethically? Is the assembly line real work? Is corporate social responsibility good?

Some people think that Christians consider making a profit unethical. And that they cannot be active in business, as it pursues selfish ends. In fact, the contrary is true: profit is important for the survival, life, and flourishing of businesses and therewith of society. Jesus encouraged his disciples to accept a just reward in return for their toiling *(Lk 10:7)*. But profit can never be the sole guiding principle. When measuring the success of a business, you should also take into account how much it contributes to society and to what extent it has an eye for everyone concerned.

In other words, businesses are expected to serve the common good, not only profit. Christian business owners make use of their God-given talents to run their business as well as they can *(Mt 25:14-30)*. This can be done through various business models, as long as the fundamental principles of human dignity, subsidiarity, solidarity and the common good are applied *(see Basics)*. Thus business activity can contribute to the realisation of the kingdom of God, which begins here *(Lk 17:21)*.

Satisfaction

Good relationships with clients, suppliers, subcontractors, experts, and especially employees are essential for the success of competitive business. Proper relationships respect the human dignity of others, and seek to help people flourish. Cutting costs and streamlining efficiency are important ways to increase profit. But often these measures are at odds with the joy and dignity of work. For example, assembly lines have been set up with the aim of producing more in less time. The result may be that workers no longer feel included in the production of a product of which they can be proud. They only repeat a rather dull action or movement over and over again. Does such work correspond with human dignity and the satisfaction provided by dignified work?

Live and let live?

Subsidiarity is a fundamental principle wherever people interact *(see Basics)*. In a company it basically means that what can be done and decided by people on the work floor should not be done by higher management. Subsidiarity means that everyone can and should take their personal responsibility. It is more than 'live and let live', which has a connotation of disinterest. The intention of subsidiarity is that at every level in the organisation people can do real and meaningful work, and that they are supported by higher levels to do their tasks as they know them best.

There is an element of service here: just as Jesus knelt to wash the feet of his disciples *(Jn 13:2-15)*, the management is at the service of those at a lower level. All work together, each at their own level, to deliver good products or services. For example, to be effective, the protection of the environment cannot just be left to the government, but should be a key issue at every level in an organisation. The same applies to fighting forced (child) labour, exploitation of people, animal cruelty...

Corporate social responsibility

Corporate social responsibility (CSR) refers to a business approach that helps a company monitor its impact on society in the broadest sense: economic, social, environmental... Practising integrity at work is very biblical *(Lk 3:10-14)*. CSR intends to serve both the community and the company, improve the relationship between employees and employers, and consider the work in relation to society. The impact of CSR varies a lot, depending on the honest motivation of the company. Critics refer to CSR as unnecessary window-dressing, for economic purpose should be ethical and socially effective without CSR. Still, it is great if such initiatives help companies to pursue a more ethical and moral business strategy in line with the Christian ideal.

EXPLORE

Option for the marginalised

When businesses flourish, the first to benefit should be the poor *(see Question 1)*. In fact, in the past century or so, the economic situation of many people has advanced drastically. Between the 'classes' of the rich and the poor there is a great middle mass of people who can afford reasonably comfortable lives, thanks to their share in making the social economic motor run.

This good progress needs to continue, for many people are still marginalised. New opportunities must be created to give these people a share in the global economic progress. The fundamental option for the poor goes further than paying taxes that are used for social projects or donating money to charity: it is a commitment that should penetrate every economic activity and business enterprise.

READ MORE

#TwGOD 4.48; #OnlineSaints 1.13.
Business: CCC 2432; CCCC 516;
YOUCAT 428, 443; DOCAT 163, 184-190.

PRAY

God our father, inspire me to contribute to the common good through my work, in line with my vocation, and always adhere to the highest moral principles.

More than growth alone

Service to the common good includes care for God's creation *(Gen 2:15)* and solidarity with the needy *(Lk 14:13)*. Obviously, a business cannot give everything away if it is to continue to operate. But economic growth is not its only motivating factor. A good example of solidarity could be to employ people in the margins of the employment market: elderly unemployed people, disabled people, rehabilitated prisoners... Every business endeavour is related to the common good of all, and thus transcends the sole pursuit of profit.

QUOTE

Businesses serve the common good

Subsidiarity: "Just as it is gravely wrong to take from individuals what they can accomplish by their own initiative and industry and give it to the community, so also it is an injustice and at the same time a grave evil and disturbance of right order to assign to a greater and higher association what lesser and subordinate organisations can do. For every social activity ought of its very nature to furnish help to the members of the body social, and never destroy and absorb them." **[Pope Pius XI, Quadragesimo Anno, 79]**

"The purpose of a business firm is not simply to make a profit, but is to be found in its very existence as a community of persons who in various ways are endeavouring to satisfy their basic needs, and who form a particular group at the service of the whole of society. Profit is a regulator of the life of a business, but it is not the only one; other human and moral factors must also be considered." **[Pope John Paul II, Centesimus Annus, 35]**

"The dignity of each human person and the pursuit of the common good are concerns which ought to shape all economic policies... Business is a vocation, and a noble vocation, provided that those engaged in it see themselves challenged by a greater meaning in life; this will enable them truly to serve the common good by striving to increase the goods of this world and to make them more accessible to all."

[Pope Francis, Evangelii Gaudium, 203]

SAINT

Christian business owner

The approach of the medieval businessman Homobonus is remarkably accurate for today's standards. Care for people, integrity in the broadest sense, and a striving for excellence were all part of his approach. This successful entrepreneur managed to fully integrate his faith in his work, and he solved every new moral question together with the Lord.

THINK

- Is ambition wrong? Why (not)?
- Should the Church be concerned with economic and business questions? Why (not)?
- What is the best basis for solving moral dilemmas?
- How do you imagine the ideal Christian business?

How to act ethically at work

At work, you will be confronted with possibly difficult moral dilemmas. Your faith and the principles presented in this book can help you come to a good decision every time.

- Suppose you have to choose between losing your job and doing something that harms people or the environment. Christ has taught you to love your fellow human beings. But there may also be loved ones who depend on the income you generate with your job. But then, the Bible tells us that sometimes we have to accept suffering for a greater good *(1 Pt 4:12-13)*. What decision will allow you to sleep at night without a feeling of guilt?
- Can a Christian work for government organisations that send back immigrants to their countries? *(see Question 3)*. And what about tobacco companies, intelligence agencies, weapon manufacturers, lawyers defending murderers...?
- Should a sportsman refuse to play in a stadium which was constructed by underpaid and maltreated people? Mistreating people is always wrong. But now that the stadium is finished should you not honour their hard work by making use of what they built? *(see Question 16)*. Or would your presence there be seen as a silent acceptance of their fate?
- What if your boss is committing fraud, using also the results of your work. Does that mean you are involved? Should you report them, or let it be? Should you talk to them first?

The answer cannot be given in general. It is in the specific situation that you will need to weigh the arguments, possibly asking advice from someone you trust, and come to a personal decision in faith.

Christian businesses are driven by the principle of love, dignity of work, and social responsibility. Your conscience will help you distinguish right from wrong.

Is a sustainable economy possible?

Can we limit state intervention? Are capitalism, consumerism and technological advancement diabolic? Why should I pay taxes?

The economy exists for the sake of people: we do not live for the economy. Jesus said that we cannot serve God and wealth *(Mt 6:24)*. Economic life should never become a 'survival of the fittest' at the expense of the weak, small, and poor. In fact, the living conditions of the smallest in society are an important indicator of the success of an economy! Especially when emergency aid is accompanied by measures that help those who can work to find employment *(see Question 16)*.

The free market is important for companies to develop initiatives and search for new ways to make a profit. At the same time, government regulation is needed to ensure the rights and wellbeing of all, especially the marginalised. This cannot be achieved through self-regulation of the market alone. All need to contribute to gradually realise the ideal of heaven on earth for all.

Principles for economic activity

There is not one perfect economic model for Christians. But some foundational principles need to be upheld at all times *(see Basics)*. The principle of human dignity is fundamental for every economy *(see Question 1)*. When applied to the market, the principle of subsidiarity leaves companies free to develop their economic activities and work towards a just profit *(see Question 18)*. But the government needs to step in to ensure the social and moral rights of all. Every human being has a social dimension expressed in the principle of solidarity *(see Question 1)*. Personal and communal decisions must take into account the common good. Think of the biblical landowner who deliberately left some grain in the field for the poor *(Ruth 2:15-16)*. A social security net is needed to pick up those who miss the economic ship. For this, again government intervention is needed.

Freedom and regulation

Both freedom and regulation are needed for a successful economy that respects the dignity of all. Maybe a glimpse at two opposites can help. If a fully regulated socialist system means complete state control that prevents individual initiative and private property, it does not honour these principles. Similarly, if a fully free capitalist market means a singular focus on the maximisation of profits, it will not be able to comply with the principles. But with some adjustments – and government intervention – the capitalist system can be made to work reasonably well.

Sustainable economy

In the Christian view, a sustainable economy strives for the greatest general wellbeing of all members of society through the least use of resources and environmental harm. It is impossible to look at the economy only on a local level. No business or initiative can be entirely self-sufficient: it has an impact locally and further away *(see Question 12)*. A sustainable economy therefore takes a global view, and asks questions that go beyond efficiency and profit. For example, is it better to refine my raw materials close to the source at the other side of the world, or should I haul these bulk materials home so as to ensure employment for my people? Arguments in the order of efficiency, charity, economy, ecology all need to be part of our decision making.

EXPLORE

Should I pay taxes?

The law states that you must pay taxes, but will your money be used well? When Jesus was asked this question, he looked at the head of state depicted on money and said: "Give to the emperor the things that are the emperor's" *(Mk 12:17)*. Things in his time were certainly no better than now, and the government used the taxes for noble as well as for ungodly causes. Still, Jesus saw no problem in people paying their taxes. It would probably have been the end of civil society if he had!

At your level as a tax payer, you usually cannot escape your civil duty and have to diligently pay your taxes. What will be done with these is beyond your control. However, note that Jesus added that what is within your control is to give "to God the things that are God's" *(Mk 12:17)*. If you dedicate yourself to serving God and your neighbour, you make a proper contribution to society in a Christian sense. And of course you should do what you can to convince the government to change unjust laws or unethical use of community money *(see Question 21)*.

READ MORE

#TwGOD 4.48; #OnlineSaints 1.45.
Taxes & Economy:
CCC 2240, 2409 & 2425-2426;
CCCC 464, 508 & 512; YOUCAT 431 & 442;
DOCAT 182-183 & 158-162, 171-181.

PRAY

Dear God, you made me as a member of society. Help me to be an active player in our economy with a great eye for the underprivileged and your creation.

Consumerism

An economic system that thrives on growth alone will stimulate the buying of goods and services in ever-increasing amounts. This consumerism is contrary to the sustainable economy we want to strive for as Christians. When a few nations consume most of the resources and produce of the world, not much is left for people in other countries! *(see Question 6)*. The ever-increasing demand on resources and the subsequent processing harms the environment, and so does the throw-away culture that accompanies consumerism *(see Question 5)*. In addition, it can lead to health problems like obesity and heart failure. Reduction, repairing, and recycling are ways to go against the tide *(see Question 6)*. If you change your behaviour in this sense, you will make a real difference in the fight against the consequences of consumerism on a global scale!

QUOTE

Just economies

"What is being proposed as an alternative is not the socialist system, which in fact turns out to be state capitalism, but rather a society of free work, of enterprise and of participation. Such a society is not directed against the market, but demands that the market be appropriately controlled by the forces of society and by the state, so as to guarantee that the basic needs of the whole of society are satisfied."

[Pope John Paul II, Centesimus Annus, 35]

"The global market has stimulated first and foremost, on the part of rich countries, a search for areas in which to outsource production at low cost with a view to reducing the prices of many goods... These processes have led to a downsizing of social security systems... with consequent grave danger for the rights of workers, for fundamental human rights and for solidarity... The primary capital to be safeguarded and valued is man, the human person in his or her integrity: 'Man is the source, the focus and the aim of all economic and social life.'"

[Pope Benedict XVI, Caritas in Veritate, 25]

SAINT

Business with God

When their business crashed and her husband died, Elizabeth Seton fell into a depression. But for the sake of her children she pulled herself together with a renewed trust in God. She started to teach young ladies in New York. Her new business endeavour went well, until she chose to become a Catholic. As a consequence she lost her clients and her friends. But instead of letting herself be stopped, this enterprising woman then founded a Catholic school, together with a Congregation to run it.

THINK

- Must Christians reject economic growth as bad? Can it continue endlessly? Why (not)?
- What businesses are successful in your country? Why? Is that moral?
- Do you like money? Would you like to get more? Can you do so ethically?
- Is it a sin not to pay your taxes? Why (not)?

ACT

Is technological advancement wrong?

The use of technological equipment to assist people in their duties is a good thing, right? We no longer live in the stone age, and humanity has developed these great ways of advancing the world. But there are other issues to consider.

- The large scale use of technology since the 19th century leads to many new jobs, even today. However, this does not automatically mean an increase of dignified work *(see Question 18)*.
- Technology can save lives in hospitals, and is a great alternative for certain tedious or dangerous jobs. It can drastically reduce the costs of production, especially because fewer people are needed to produce more. On the other hand, it replaces mainly unskilled workers: what will they do now?
- Technological development should serve people, but it would seem that increasingly people are serving technology. Take for example 'techno-dependents' checking their phones all day. Is that a good development?
- Technology has a huge impact on humanity. For example, what does the digitalisation of social life mean for inter-human relationships?

As technology develops, we will be faced by many new possibilities, but also by new questions that will need to be answered on the basis of Christian principles.

RECAP

Freedom and regulation are both needed for sustainability. Regulated capitalism and technological advancement can work, but consumerism never. Tax payment is a Christian duty.

YOUR
NEIGHBOUR
IS GOD

POLITICS & STATE

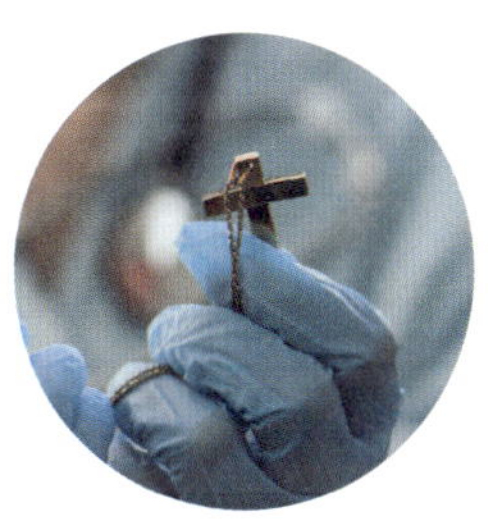

How are family, society and state related?

Does social media disrupt families? Why should I care about world news if I already care for my neighbour?

Politics & State

God did not create people for solitary life: he intended them as companions *(Gen 2:18)*. He told the first couple to go and multiply *(Gen 1:28; see #TwGOD 4.20)*. God created us out of love and for love, a love that needs to be shared. We are social beings, and only in relationship with others can we develop our full potential. Family life is our first experience of community. Here we grow up and are educated. Hence the importance of striving for stable families with a loving father and mother *(see #TwGOD 4.19)*.

Saint Paul said that we are all united in one body with many parts *(1 Cor 12:12–31)*. All are different and have a different task, but we do belong to the same body, which is the body of Christ. This is an image of the community or society, but also of the family *(see #TwGOD 2.1)*. All members have a duty to participate in family life according to their abilities. This is the basis of their (later) participation in society *(see Question 21)*. At a certain moment in life, we leave our family and possibly start one ourselves. Whatever we do, our experience of family has a great influence on who we are and how we act.

Society: community

Every family is a small society in itself. Society then is firstly an accumulation of family cells, a community built up from small communities. Jesus grew up in a loving family, and formed a growing community of Christians. Even the single people in a society come from a family, and hopefully maintain a certain bond with their family. As such, families are the foundational bricks on which a society is built. The Church teaches: "Authority, stability, and a life of relationships within the family constitute the foundations for freedom, security, and fraternity within society" *(CCC 2207)*.

State: peace and justice

In its best form, society is a community of individuals in continuous social interaction. This is different from the state, which is the politically organised community in a given territory. The

EXPLORE

Social media: disruptive or constructive?

There are many great ways in which social networks can help people to be connected. Online communications media offer wonderful opportunities. Distances no longer count in sharing joys or griefs, uniting in prayer, or offering advice. A wealth of information is available at our fingertips. Imagine if Jesus had been able to use these tools for his mission...

But there also is the horror image of a family dinner where kids and parents are each focused on their private screen, mindlessly munching away in silence. In a TED talk, Pope Francis said that none of us is an island and that we need to stand together *(26 Apr. 2017)*. Family time is precious and should allow for true human contact and conversation. This means having to learn when to put your screen down. Just as families teach their children to cross the road safely and not to take sweets from strangers, they should also learn how to avoid the pitfalls and dangers of online media.

The tools in themselves are neither good nor evil; it is the use we make of them that will determine whether they are disruptive or constructive. We can use these media to do immense good to the world, sharing Jesus' good news with everyone on the planet! He calls us to do so wherever we are, also as online missionaries! *(see Question 26)*.

members of society elect a government to help organise social life within the state. Outwardly, the government relates to other states. Assuring peace, freedom and justice are primary tasks of the state. The peaceful living together in society is closely related to social justice *(see Question 10 & 14)*.

Who does what?

Both state and family have their own responsibilities and tasks. The state should not intervene in areas of social life that pertain to the family, while individual families should follow the just laws of the state. The relationship between state and family is regulated by the principle of subsidiarity, which states that a higher authority should not do or decide what can be done on a lower level *(see Basics)*. For example, the state cannot decide what religion a child should have, or how many children a family can have *(see Question 9)*. But the state should ensure educational opportunities for all children, and guarantee freedom of religion *(see Question 23)*.

READ MORE

#TwGOD 4.19, 4.47; #OnlineSaints 1.21-1.22.
Family & State: CCC 2196-2233 & 2234-2243;
CCCC 455-462 & 463-465; YOUCAT 367-374 & 375-377;
DOCAT 112-128 & 131-133, 198-200.

PRAY

Father of all, help me to contribute
to the society in which I live,
first of all by living my faith in my
family and personal environment.

Solidarity through taxes

'Why should my taxes pay for the nursing home of parents whose well-off children refuse to pay for their care?' There are many variations of this question, which expresses the sense of injustice we feel when society has to pay for costs that could or should be covered by individuals or families.

To come to an answer, we can turn the question around. Should society abandon people who are abandoned by their own? While justice demands that those who shun their (family) duty should be reprimanded or punished, mercy and solidarity demand that we help those who are marginalised or in need *(see Question 1)*.

QUOTE

The family

"The first and fundamental structure for 'human ecology' is the family, in which man receives his first formative ideas about truth and goodness, and learns what it means to love and to be loved, and thus what it actually means to be a person. Here we mean the family founded on marriage, in which the mutual gift of self by husband and wife creates an environment in which children can be born and develop their potentialities, become aware of their dignity and prepare to face their unique and individual destiny."

[Pope John Paul II, Centesimus Annus, 39]

"If a family uses [online media] to be more connected, to then meet at table and look into each other's eyes, then it is a resource. If a Church community coordinates its activity through the social network, and then celebrates the Eucharist together, then it is a resource... This is the social network we want, a network created not to entrap, but to liberate... where unity is based not on 'likes', but on the truth, on the 'Amen', by which each one clings to the Body of Christ, and welcomes others."

[Pope Francis, World Communications Day, 24 Jan. 2019]

SAINT

Pillars of society

Like countless other couples, Luigi and Maria Quattrocchi founded a family. They took seriously their role in the community of society. Both worked consciously for the bettering of the situation of certain groups in society, and played a fundamental role in institutions like the Italian scouts and Catholic Action. While they knew they could not do everything, they also knew that God counted on their contribution to society.

THINK

- Are you proud of the society you live in? Why (not)?
- Should the state have more power or less? Why?
- Would it be a good idea to found a fully Christian state somewhere far away?
- Must the state support families with children in any particular way? How?

ACT

Should I care about the world news?

When you follow the international news, it may seem to be a continuous sequence of violence, war, suffering, disaster... So why bother following it?

- It looks like history repeats itself over and again, only people and places are different. But those people and places are precisely what makes the news different today: it is about people who are your brothers and sisters, and who are suffering at this very moment. Would you not like to know what happens to your siblings, even if you may receive bad news?
- 'It is enough for me to follow the local news', you may hear people say. But is the love for neighbour that Jesus taught you only for those in your close vicinity? Or is the community of your brothers and sisters larger? All of them are part of the global society we form together.
- 'It makes me feel sad to watch the news.' Yes, the world is not yet the perfect place that God wants for us. But does the suffering go away if you ignore it? There is always something you can do: in any case you can pray for those in need! That is in itself a very good reason to follow the news.
- Following the news regularly helps you to increase your understanding. You will start to see how the economic and political situation in the world influences the wellbeing of people. It will also help you to see how human relations shape our society. Do you think this can help you to become closer to them, and maybe even to God?

For Christians, there are many reasons to get out of our bubble and follow the news, especially when we let it enter our relationship with God. Obviously, it is important to separate the reporter's opinion from the facts when following news reports. A critical approach will help you recognise fake news quickly and form your personal view.

RECAP

Founded on family cells, society is organised politically and economically in the state. If used well, social media are a great gift. Charity includes following the news about others.

Can I join politics?

Must I vote? How can I decide whom to vote for? Are Christians better politicians?

Politics & State

The dirty games and untruths that seem to rule part of the political scene are far from the Christian view on life and society. And so are many of the political positions voiced. This is why some people claim Christians should stay away from politics. Did Jesus not tell us to search only for the kingdom of God and his righteousness? *(Mt 6:33)*. However, by virtue of our existence, we are also members of the society in which we live *(see Question 20)*. It is the calling of each individual to participate in its social life, also through politics.

Participation

The Catholic principle of participation means that every person contributes to society *(see Basics)*. This is true no matter what and how you are. In fact, participation does not start by doing but by being yourself. A poor member participates no less than a rich one, a physically or mentally challenged person no less than anyone else. This is because each human being is willed and loved by God himself. Helping the needy, supporting sports or culture, defending the oppressed or the environment, voting, standing for political office: these are just a few examples of participation. We all have different gifts, and should use these in accordance with our personal vocation *(Rom 12:4-8)*. You can find this vocation deep in your own heart through prayer, by following your very deepest desire *(see #TwGOD 4.4)*. Jesus said that Christians should be the salt of the earth and the light of the world: also in politics we must do what we can to advance his cause *(Mt 5:13-16)*.

Politics

An important way in which the wellbeing of our society can be promoted is through politics. It allows us to participate in the just organisation of our human community. Pope Francis warned that "when political life is not seen as a form of service to society as a whole, it can become a means of oppression,

EXPLORE

Christian politicians

There is a great need for good Christian politicians. Even apart from specifically religious or moral themes, we have so much to offer to the world! If we truly believe in what we teach, we also believe that the Christian contribution is for the good of all humanity. True Christian politics is always in line with the Bible and the teaching of the Church. What that means in practice is not always easy to discern. Therefore a Christian politician first of all needs a living faith, and a prayerful relationship with God to fall back on.

'What would Jesus do?' is a good question in any situation where you try to give a Christian answer to a new situation. Not always can this answer be directly found in the Bible. That is precisely why it is important to get to know Jesus intimately: a solid Christian politician is a close disciple of Jesus, and lives their political office as a divine vocation. A good understanding of the social teaching of the Church is of course important too, and will help them to take a stance in line with their faith and conscience in every situation.

Sadly, not all Christian politicians are as upright and credible as they should be. But that should not discourage you to try to do better. As Pope Francis said, even if you were to stumble as a politician and get your hands dirty, do not give up, but sincerely ask forgiveness and go forward! *(30 Apr. 2015).*

marginalisation and even destruction" *(1 Jan. 2019).* Politics can be a high vocation and even a great form of charity when politicians respect the life, freedom, and dignity of all people in society.

 # Vote and serve

Christians can and should participate in politics. First of all by voting in accordance with our consciences. If all options are morally impossible, casting a blank vote may be a way to express our participation. Some Christians are called to join the political arena themselves. They voice their political position in line with God's teachings – helped by the principles of the social teaching of the Church *(see Basics).* It is very important that Christians are active in politics, and those who do so diligently deserve our support, as they face an extremely complicated task. Often, it will be very difficult to find a political compromise that still respects the foundational teachings of the faith. This is true for voters and politicians alike *(see Explore).*

READ MORE

#TwGOD 4.48; #OnlineSaints 1.42.
Politics & Participation: CCC 1901, 2442 & 1913-1917;
CCCC 406, 519 & 410; YOUCAT 440-441;
DOCAT 195-197, 201-213, 219, 319 & 98-99.

PRAY

Dear Lord, help me to understand your desire for the common good of all people and teach me to contribute my share to the political life of society.

Jesus the politician?

Jesus could easily have started a revolution to overthrow an unjust regime. But he taught peace and non-violence *(Mt 5:44)*. He could have told his followers to refuse to pay taxes. But he did the contrary *(Mt 22:21)*. The people wanted to crown him king, but he escaped to a mountain *(Jn 6:15)*. When Pontius Pilate questioned him about his political stance, he explained: "My kingdom is not of this world" *(Jn 18:36)*. With these words Jesus distanced himself from earthly politics. He came to announce us God's rule, which is very different from that of any earthly government. Jesus wanted to show us the way to the Kingdom of heaven, where the highest rule is love.

QUOTE

A high calling

"To take politics seriously at its different levels - local, regional, national and worldwide - is to affirm the duty of man, of every man, to recognise the concrete reality and the value of the freedom of choice that is offered to him to seek to bring about both the good of the city and of the nation and of mankind. Politics are a demanding manner - but not the only one - of living the Christian commitment to the service of others... While recognising the autonomy of the reality of politics, Christians who are invited to take up political activity should try to make their choices consistent with the Gospel."

[Pope Paul VI, Octogesima Adveniens, 46]

"Catholics know well that 'in concrete situations, and taking into account the solidarity that each one lives, it is necessary to recognise a legitimate variety of possible options. The same Christian faith can lead to different commitments.' Therefore, I invite you to live your faith with great freedom. Without believing that there is a single form of political commitment for Catholics."

[Pope Francis, To young Latin American leaders, 4 March 2019]

SAINT

Pray and rule

Cunegunde married the future emperor of the Holy Roman Empire, Henry II. The devout couple prayed together and ruled together. Henry involved her in all important decisions, and they greatly advanced the just relationship between Church and state. He was a decisive political ruler, who stood for his Catholic principles, sought union with his enemies, and brought peace in his realm.

THINK

- Did you vote in the last election? Do you think this is important for Christians? Why (not?)
- Do you think what politicians say in campaigns is what they truly stand for? Why (not)?
- Do you know who represents you in your government? Is that important?
- Has democracy changed in the past decades? For better or worse? How?

ACT

Is there a Christian way to vote?

There absolutely is, and it demands some investment from your side to make up your mind in accordance with the teaching of your faith: you will want to find out which candidate best promotes justice and the common good. Some considerations.

- Morals over money: Are you ready to vote for a candidate who will abolish the tax advantages you are enjoying in order to privilege people in the margins of society?
- Vote strategically: Should you vote for that small faction with a clear pro-life stance, knowing they will not make it into government? Or should you better help advance that other party with principles that are also acceptable for Christians, and which with a few more votes will govern?
- Vote Christian: A specific Christian political party can be a good choice, but you do not have to vote for them if in conscience you find another party which better promotes the Christian stance in a global sense.
- Asking 'What would Jesus do?' can often be useful, but may pose problems as many of today's issues are not addressed directly in the Bible. The Tradition and the social teaching of the Church as expressed in this book can help.

When preparing to cast your vote for a person or party, you need to consider all their views, intentions, and strategies. In doing so, you will probably discover that none of the candidates is perfect. So, how to vote? On a positive note, try to see which candidate does most for humanity. Put negatively, choose the lesser evil. Above all, pray, and decide with God in conscience.

RECAP

Christians are called to be actively involved in politics, first of all by voting in accordance to their conscience. The world needs great Christian politicians.

Are state and Church not separate?

So why does the Church join the political debate? Should priests tell us how to vote? Can I disagree with the government?

Church and state each have their proper role to play. 'Church' in this context involves the entire Church community, and 'state' ideally includes all of members of society. In practice the dialogue between Church and state is realised by the leaders of the respective institutions. Saint Augustine thought a lot about the 'earthly city' (the state) and the 'city of God' (the Church community) *(see Saint)*. For him, the state should strive for peace in order to prepare earth for the establishment of a heavenly city *(De Civitate Dei, XIX.17)*.

The state is necessarily temporary, as one day – at the end of times – God's heavenly power will take over directly. Pope Gelasius later spoke of two swords. The temporal sword of the government rules with natural authority for the common good of the community. The Church yields the spiritual sword and exercises its supernatural authority for the spiritual welfare of the community. So the Church both works for the common good of all at this moment, and shows them the way to eternal life with God after this life.

Meddling or caring?

The Church has a sacred duty to work for the 'salvation of souls' by telling everyone of the great message of Jesus *(Mt 28:19)*. That the Church has an opinion about everything is not the result of nosy meddling, but of genuine care for the present and future wellbeing of all! Saint Paul said that our citizenship is in heaven *(Phil 3:20)*, a citizenship which we exercise now here on earth as members of society. When the Church speaks about political themes, it does so for the good of humanity.

A secular state

If secular rulers were to listen perfectly to their human conscience, their decisions would be just and right – even without reference to religion. This is because every human being carries deep in themselves traces of God who created them. This explains the general agreement among peoples about certain universal human rights *(see Question 13)*. A secular state should remain neutral in matters of religion, treating everyone equally regardless of religion. At the same time, it should promote the freedom of every individual to exercise the religion of their choice. Unfortunately, this is not always applied in reality *(see Question 23)*. Such a secular state is different from a secularism which promotes atheism or aims at the deconstruction of religion.

Authority in the Bible

Jesus distinguished between the authority of God and the secular authority when he said that the disciples should "give to the emperor the things that are the emperor's, and to God the things that are God's" *(Mt 22:21; see Question 20)*. This means we are to comply with civil law, whether we like it or not. Saint Peter told us to accept the rule of human institutions *(1 Pt 2:13-15)*. But Scripture also teaches us to "obey God rather than any human authority" *(Acts 5:29)*. We cannot obey the government if it tells us to go against the laws of God! But we can and should always pray for our rulers *(1 Tim 2:1-2)*.

READ MORE

#TwGOD 2.1, 2.6, 2.45-2.48; #OnlineSaints 1.44.
Society & Church: CCC 1878-1904 & 2032-2040, 2244-2246, 2420-2421; CCCC 401-406 & 430, 510; YOUCAT 322-326 & 344; DOCAT 18, 305-316 & 31-33, 220-225.

EXPLORE

Can Church leaders tell me how to vote?

Voting is an important expression of your personal participation in society *(see Question 21)*. Everyone should be free to vote in accordance with their consciences. Again the principle of subsidiarity applies: that which can be done or decided by community members themselves should not be taken from them by any authority *(see Basics)*. So, Church leaders cannot and should not tell you whom to vote for.

That said, you have a sacred duty to 'inform your conscience', to do what you can to find out which is the best way to vote as a Christian in the given situation. While Church leaders can help people form their conscience (without telling them exactly how to vote), priests may not be the best political advisers in the community. Certain lay community members will have much more experience in this regard. In fact, priests are forbidden to share in the exercise of civil power, so they cannot hold public office. They have another vocation! Lay Christians however can and should stand for office if they feel this is their vocation. They can try to convince their fellow Catholics to vote for them, but they too have to respect the freedom of conscience of each individual.

PRAY

Father almighty, help us to serve you and our brothers and sisters in society also through politics, basing ourselves on what we learn from you for the good of all.

Is democracy Christian?

Some claim that democracy is a Christian invention. It is not. The term was coined by the ancient Greeks. Although much can be said against our democratic systems of today, if served honestly they are better than many alternatives. The idea of giving power to the people is in line with the principles of subsidiarity and personal freedom, but there is the danger of majority formations. A majority group should not move forward like a steamroller crushing the needs and opinions of those who do not share the majority views. Therefore, in the Christian view, a democracy should always apply the principle of solidarity as well, defending the rights of minority groups and marginalised people.

QUOTE

Two spheres

"There are two powers... by which the world is governed, the sacred authority of the priesthood and the power of kings. Of these the priestly is by so much the greater as they will have to answer for kings themselves in the day of divine judgement."

[Pope Gelasius, To Emperor Anastasius, c. 494 AD]

"The just ordering of society and the state is a central responsibility of politics... Fundamental to Christianity is... the distinction between Church and state... The state may not impose religion, yet it must guarantee religious freedom and harmony between the followers of different religions. For her part, the Church, as the social expression of Christian faith, has a proper independence and is structured on the basis of her faith as a community which the state must recognise. The two spheres are distinct, yet always interrelated... A just society must be the achievement of politics, not of the Church. Yet the promotion of justice through efforts to bring about openness of mind and will to the demands of the common good is something which concerns the Church deeply."

[Pope Benedict XVI, Deus Caritas Est, 28]

SAINT

Love and do what you will

Augustine contributed a lot to the thinking about the relationship between Church and state. Ultimately, his political and moral position can be summarised in his words "Love, and do what you will" *(Sermon on 1 Jn)*. He did not come to the faith easily, and struggled greatly with sin and doubt before he found peace. In that he is just like us and our politicians!

THINK

- Can public money be used to fund religious initiatives? Why (not)?
- Should the state promote a moment of silence before meals, so those who wish can pray? Why (not)?
- Should the Church have the freedom to 'discriminate' when it desires to employ only Christians, for example? Why (not)?
- Would you like to receive advice on how to vote? From whom?

ACT

Disagree or participate?

You may disagree with the course the government is taking.

- However, this does not give you the right to lethargically withdraw from participation in politics. Rather, if you think that things are going wrong in your country that is another reason to let your voice or vote be heard, always in such a way that you apply the highest principle of love. How could you do so in daily life?
- Your most important guiding light is your conscience. Deep in yourself the answer can be found. That is because you are a creature of God, and as such carry part of his truth in yourself. The Holy Spirit, the great inspirer, wants to help you listen to your conscience. The best way to learn to do so is by praying and getting to know God's view of the world better. Do you wish to grow closer to God in this way?
- Christians continue to stand on high moral ground even when all seems lost, simply because we cannot serve anything but the truth, which is found in Jesus *(Jn 8:31-32)*. That gives us strength and integrity, but also makes us vulnerable as our opponents know exactly what we stand for. This is yet another reason to get involved and support that worthy candidate. Did you ever look at your role in politics in this way?

Whatever happens, the Bible instructs us to pray for our political leaders *(1 Tim 2:1-2)*, which should be our first way of participating.

RECAP

The Church speaks up in favour of the common good, but leaves individuals free to choose how to vote. You can disagree with the government if you let your conscience guide you.

Can public officials wear religious symbols?

May the state limit (religious) freedom? Could a Christian be a nationalist, defect or support another state?

Politics & State

The displaying of religious symbols like crosses in public spaces sometimes leads to heated debates. Should a historically Christian country which wishes to treat all religions equally remove all these symbols, at least from government buildings *(see Question 13)*? But that would also mean effacing history, and possibly forgetting that the fundamental principles of this society come from a particular religious outlook on humankind and the world *(see Question 20)*.

Right to believe

A similar debate asks whether public officials can wear external symbols of their faith. This is not only related to the desire to promote a secular state, but also to the fundamental right of freedom of religion. For example, when a Christian wears a small cross around their neck, or a Muslim wears a headscarf without endangering themselves or others, why would the government have the right to limit them in their fundamental right of freedom to choose and exercise their religion? This debate is further complicated when certain religious symbols not only express the religion of the wearer, but are also claimed by certain groups as a political statement.

You may wonder whether we really need such symbols. As God is immaterial, and our future is with him, why bother about material objects to express our faith? In heaven we do not need these. But we are not only spirit: we also have a material body with material needs. God gave us the capacity to touch, see, smell, hear, and taste. Each of these senses can serve in our relationship with God. During the liturgy in church all the senses are addressed *(see #TwGOD 3.24)*. Material objects like a small cross or rosary can be very helpful to remind you of your relationship with God during the hectic pace of everyday life. You should be free to wear and use these as you deem fit.

Social order or censorship?

There are many ways in which a state rightly limits the exercise of freedoms by its inhabitants *(see Question 13)*. This is the only way to assure a social order with basic freedoms for all. But there is a fine line between a just reduction of rights for the common good, and state censorship.

A good example is the just prohibition to smoke in certain places in order to protect the health of non-smokers. But can the government prohibit smoking all together in order to protect smokers against themselves? On the one hand it is important to prevent that young girl from falling into the pitfall of a smoking addiction. But is it fair that the 80-year-old man for whom his quiet Sunday cigar is one of the few highlights of the week can no longer afford that simple pleasure because of increased taxes or total prohibition? And what about his freedom of choice?

Justice for all

Similarly, restricting religious groups that want to harm human beings is important, but, for example, imposing a state religion is wrong. The clashes of rights and freedoms cannot be solved by general rules alone: exceptions are needed, and rules should always be accompanied by a just care for the wellbeing of individuals and minority groups. These should always flow forth from the desire to serve the common good *(see Basics)*.

EXPLORE

Freedom and subsidiarity

An important question is just how far fundamental human rights can be limited by the state. The principle of subsidiarity can help *(see Basics)*. For example, it is great when the government strives for equal opportunities and good education for all children, but it cannot force parents to teach their child a moral framework which does not correspond with their beliefs. It pertains to the family to educate children in the faith of their choice.

The faithful must be free to express what they believe to be true and morally right without fearing to be marginalised, lose their job, or suffer violence. This is even the case if their position is considered wrong by other groups in society. For example, if certain Christians believe that shopping on Sundays should be reduced to a minimum, they must be able to say so freely, and even organise a peaceful protest. But when they start to physically attack people with shopping bags they should be stopped immediately.

It pertains to the state to watch over the equal treatment of all, and fight every form of unjust discrimination and violence. Here again it is the principle of subsidiarity that helps to ensure the fundamental rights of all.

READ MORE

#TwGOD 4.11, 4.45;
#OnlineSaints 1.43, 2.48-2.49.
Subsidiarity & Religious symbols:
CCC 1883-1885 & 2129-2132; CCCC 403 & 446;
YOUCAT 323 & 358; DOCAT 95-98.

PRAY

Dear Lord, help me to respect the fundamental rights of every human being, while fighting all forma of unjust treatment, discrimination, and violence.

Love for country or nationalism?

It is deeply human to love your home and your country. But nationalism is wrong and selfish if it means the exclusion or the detriment of the interests of other peoples or nations *(see Act)*. You may live in a country that promotes other values than those you believe in. No-one can force you to give up your values, and you should even be free to support another state – but you will still have to follow the local laws insofar as your conscience allows you. If deep in yourself you feel that you can no longer support the general rule of your country, you need to protest. Some Christians in hostile environment give great witness of their faith by staying where they are. Sometimes the only solution is to leave and find a place where you are free to believe in accordance with your conscience. For example when you live in a police state and are forced to act against your deepest conscience. Although the nation you leave behind may see this as unlawful defection, morally, leaving may be the right thing to do if you can. In all this, listening to your conscience, guided by the Holy Spirit, is essential.

QUOTE

Religious freedom and dignity

"The right to religious freedom has its foundation in the very dignity of the human person as this dignity is known through the revealed word of God and by reason itself. This right of the human person to religious freedom is to be recognised in the constitutional law whereby society is governed and thus it is to become a civil right."

[Second Vatican Council, Dignitatis Humanae, 2]

"The global dimension has to be considered without ever losing sight of the local. As a reaction to a 'spherical' notion of globalisation, one that levels differences and smooths out particularities, it is easy for forms of nationalism to re-emerge... Some of these attitudes go back to the period between the two World Wars, when populist and nationalist demands proved more forceful than the activity of the League of Nations. The reappearance of these impulses today is progressively weakening the multilateral system, resulting in a general lack of trust, a crisis of credibility in international political life, and a gradual marginalisation of the most vulnerable members of the family of nations."

[Pope Francis, To the diplomatic corps, 7 Jan. 2019]

SAINT

Peace through freedom

In his foundational book Utopia, Thomas More said that adherence to the principle of religious freedom would promote peace, also among Christians. He himself had to pay dearly for his faithfulness to his Catholic convictions when the English King turned against the Church of Rome and tried to impose other beliefs on Thomas. But Thomas remained faithful to his Catholic faith: he could not betray his conscience.

THINK

- Do you love your country? Why (not)?
- Should 'ostentatious' religious symbols be prohibited? How do you define this objectively?
- Does religious freedom require respect for other religions? Why (not)?
- Can freedom of religion for all contribute to world peace? How?

ACT

How to react to nationalism?

Nationalist and populist voices seem to be on the rise. What is the proper Christian answer?

- Some argue that only thanks to nationalism did their nations become great. But at what price? Often, entire peoples were exploited and horrible crimes committed to gain wealth unilaterally. How can we glorify that history as Christians?
- The danger of nationalism becomes very clear in ideas of the Nazis. Their blind fanaticism led to terrible suffering that still has consequences today. Is there anything Christian in this?
- Whenever we hear words like 'Our own people first', we need to be on our guard, for Jesus' message is addressed to the entire human family, not just a select group. What can you do yourself?

We conclude with the words of the Polish Pope John Paul II to his compatriots: "Love of our country unites us and must unite us above all divergences. It has nothing in common with a narrow nationalism or chauvinism, but springs from the law of the human heart" *(23 Oct. 1978)*.

RECAP

Fundamental human rights can only be limited to protect other fundamental rights. Love for country is great but nationalism is selfish. We all need to adapt to each other.

YOUR
NEIGHBOUR
IS GOD

TECHNOLOGY & FAITH SHARING

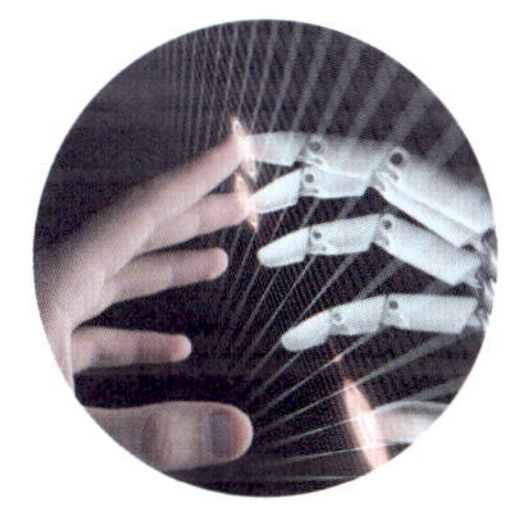

24

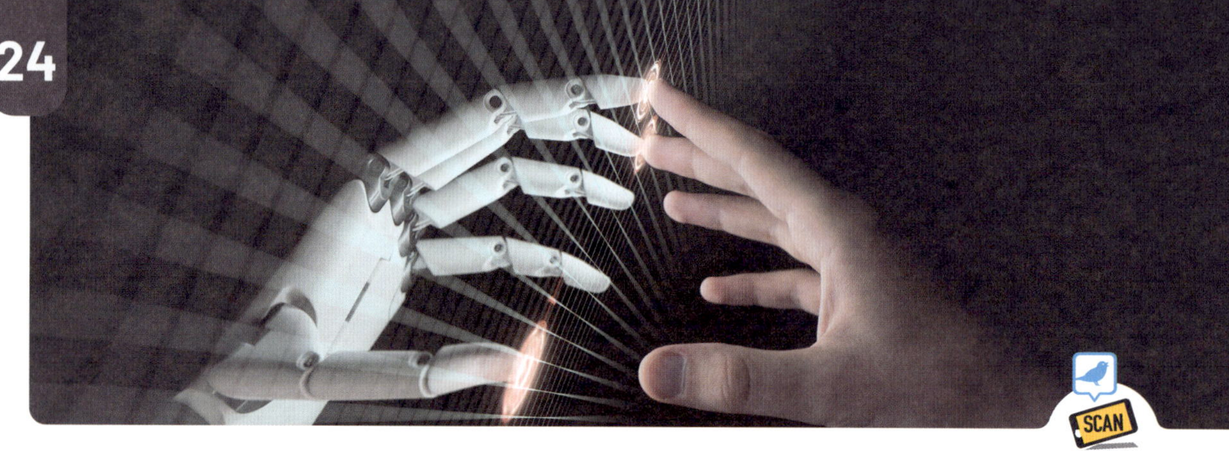

Can human embryos be used to save lives?

What is bioethics? Is artificial intelligence a blessing or a danger? What do you think about transhumanism?

No more illness, better mental and physical capacities, longer and healthier lives: we can have many dreams about an enhanced version of ourselves. The Bible promises that in heaven we will have a perfect 'glorified body' *(1 Cor 15:35-57)*. But at the moment we have to make do with our imperfect selves. Thankfully, in recent decades there have been great developments that blot out certain illnesses, help people with disabilities, and lengthen our lives. Many developments are very good, but not everything that can be done should be done. So how far can we go?

The Christian view can help to see things from the right perspective. Jesus did not take away all illness and human limits, and nor can we *(see Question 25)*. Also in this field, there is a big split between rich and poor. If certain technologies indeed improve the standards of life drastically, the principle of solidarity states that it should be made available to everyone *(see Basics)*.

The ethics of life

Bioethics is the ethics of life (*bios* in Greek). Jesus wants us to have life in abundance *(Jn 10:10)*. Human life is infinitely desired by God *(Gen 2:7)*. It is to be treasured and protected at every stage. Our life starts at conception, and only finishes at natural death *(see #TwGOD 4.26 & 4.37)*. The Catholic view on bioethics helps people make moral decisions as technologies rapidly open the way to new possibilities. Many bioethical questions can be found in the book *Tweeting with GOD (see #TwGOD 4.26-4.42)*.

Transhumanism

If by transhumanism you mean a prosthesis that replaces a lost leg, or a pacemaker that keeps someone's heart beating, then this is a great thing. Nature is not perfect, and it is marvellous when technologies can help us to function better as humans. However, transhumanism also refers to various philosophical currents that basically try to create a better version of humankind. This contradicts our faith that we are created by God and that he created us good *(Gen 1:27.31)*. If we try to turn

EXPLORE

Embryos as medicine or vaccine?

Is it ethical to use cells from human embryos in medicine? *(see #TwGOD 4.36)*. Even the smallest embryo is a precious life with a human dignity and right to live! *(see #TwGOD 4.26)*. An essential moral principle is that we cannot sacrifice a life to save another. I can decide to sacrifice my life to save someone else, like Saint Maximilian Kolbe did in a Nazi concentration camp *(see #OnlineSaints 2.27)*. But I can never force anyone – not even an embryo – to do the same.

A very dangerous area in bioethics is medical research on the basis of human embryonic cells. What is the origin of these cells? If an embryo died a natural death, the case is similar to the donation of organs after death *(see #TwGOD 4.40)*. But what about embryos obtained through in vitro fertilisation or abortion? *(see #TwGOD 4.28 & 4.34)*. If the embryo is alive, it has the right to be protected and not to be killed. If it is dead, it is still obtained in a morally unacceptable way. This leads to great moral dilemmas.

Imagine you could develop a vaccine which can keep the entire world population safe from a dangerous illness. And that you only needed to kill a few embryos to prepare this vaccine. It sounds so tempting, but the principle of the absolute sacredness of human life tells us that this is severely wrong. But what if embryos were only needed in the development phase, and that production can be done without them? Then the immorally developed vaccine could probably best celebrate the sacrifice of innocent human life by using it to save lives. The right to life of every single human being, however small or weak, is an absolute right.

ourselves into superhumans, the result is that we become not more, but less human – because we will be less like the person God intended us to be at our creation!

Eternal life

While improving and prolonging life is a good thing because life is precious, striving for physical immortality is not. Although many consider their life on earth as reasonably good, we all experience limitations and sufferings. God did not intend this imperfect life to last forever: he prepared a much better future for us! Our future life with Jesus in heaven is not a utopia like physical immortality here on earth: it is a promise to all those who respond positively to the love of God for them.

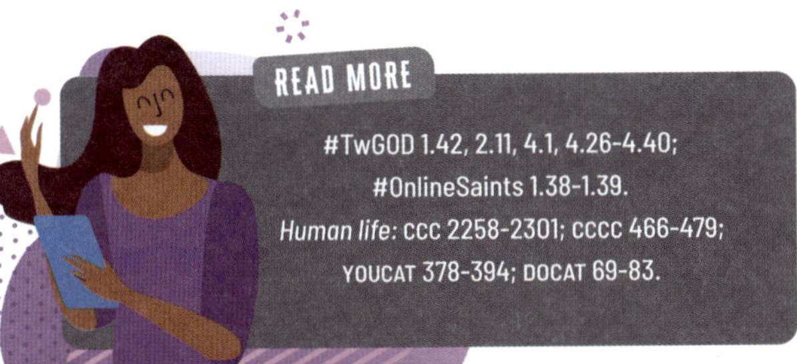

READ MORE

#TwGOD 1.42, 2.11, 4.1, 4.26-4.40;
#OnlineSaints 1.38-1.39.
Human life: CCC 2258-2301; CCCC 466-479;
YOUCAT 378-394; DOCAT 69-83.

PRAY

Dear God, help me to protect human life and use technologies to promote the dignity of all people, discerning constantly what is right in your sight.

Self-thinking machines?

It is a great use of technology when robots or drones take over dangerous human missions, like saving someone fallen off a cliff. But how is this when an armed robot or drone is sent out into enemy territory? How much discretionary ability will you give it? A human soldier confronted with a group of innocent children will hopefully listen to their conscience and hold their fire in opposition to their possibly clear orders. But can you expect a conscience in a 'self-thinking' killer bot which has to decide on the basis of a logic founded on a binary system with true/false schemes?

THINK

- Do you think technology will ever be able to eliminate death? Why (not)?
- What can you do to promote and protect human life in your environment?
- What do you think are the greatest challenges posed by transhumanist philosophies?
- Unlike technology, Jesus invites us to see beyond this life. What does that mean for you?

QUOTE

Dangers and possibilities

"The contemporary context seems to give primacy to an artificial intelligence that becomes ever more dominated by experimental techniques, and in this way forgets that all science must always safeguard man and promote his aspiration for the authentic good."

[Pope Benedict XVI, To students, 21 Oct. 2006]

"Digital innovation touches every aspect of our lives... Inequalities expand enormously; knowledge and wealth accumulate in a few hands with grave risks for democratic societies. Yet these dangers must not detract from the immense potential that new technologies offer... A critical contribution can be made by the principles of the Church's social teaching."

[Pope Francis, To the Pontifical Academy for Life, 28 Feb. 2020]

SAINT

Discernment for integral human development

Hildegard von Bingen strived for integral human development in her studies about medicine, mathematics, pharmacy, music, ethics, poetry, religion... For her, all these themes were interrelated because they all originate in God our creator. We have so many possibilities as human beings. Every time we need to discern carefully whether it is ethical to act upon our ideas or desires. Only in an intimate relationship with God is it possible to find the answer.

ACT

Artificial intelligence: a blessing or a danger?

Like all human creations, artificial intelligence (AI) is an instrument. In itself it is neither good nor bad, only its use by people can be good or bad. Here are some thoughts.

- When AI develops into an independent form of intelligence, the ethical questions do not only concern the usage made by people, but also the 'decisions' of the intelligent life itself. A robot can do things that are morally wrong, but is the robot to blame or its maker?
- When AI becomes more human-like and in some ways even more intelligent than we are, it may tempt us to reconsider what it means to be human. Although animals have some form of intelligence, humankind is of another order *(see #TwGOD 1.3)*. It is not mere intelligence that makes us human. Ultimately, we are human because God created us as such. So, can AI ever claim the same rights as humans?
- What probably distinguishes us most as humans is our will. Can a machine ever be said to have a will? We have not been programmed by God, or else our misbehaviour would be a programming mistake – which our perfect God cannot make. Our bad behaviour is the result of our free will. How does this distinguish us from AI?
- AI can successfully assist surgeons during a complex operation or make a simple diagnosis of ailments in preparation for meeting a physician. But what if AI replaces human company in a nursing home by a talking robot, for example? You could argue that at least these people have the company which the overworked nursing staff cannot give. But can AI ever offer true company?
- These are man-made machines, not creatures of God. However intelligent and independent their life may seem, can they believe in God? Are they capable of love? Can they pray? Can they be baptised?

The above shows that the development of AI makes us ask important questions, offering some true challenges to make good moral choices.

Bioethics is the ethics of life, which is infinitely precious in God's eyes. Technologies can greatly advance humanity, as long as the dignity of every human being is respected.

Why do some have everything and others nothing?

How can I live happily when they suffer? Can faith help to make sense of it all? Do I really need to convert?

At the creation, God intended the world to be a good place, but human beings chose for themselves instead of for love *(see #TwGOD 1.4)*. Since the Fall into sin of humankind, the world is an imperfect place. God suffers whenever people are poor, sick, weak and suffering. When Jesus was born, God himself became poor and weak. In Jesus, God revealed to us what it means that he is love *(1 Jn 4:8)*. In Jesus, God suffered terribly and unjustly *(1 Pt 2:21-24)*. In Jesus, God stands with the poor, weak, sick and suffering *(Lk 4:18-19)*. That is the ultimate reason for our 'option for the poor' *(see Basics)*.

There is always hope

Although he worked many miracles, Jesus did not take away all suffering, weakness, and poverty. Nor can we. When his good friend Lazarus was sick, Jesus said this illness would help to show God's greatness *(Jn 11:4)*. We know that each of us will die one day. Thankfully, there is Jesus' promise of our future life with him in heaven, where things will be perfect at last. This promise changes our outlook here on earth, and makes suffering a little more bearable. We never need to despair, for there is always the hope of a better life. Jesus wants us to tell everyone about this great news *(Mk 16:15)*.

God needs you!

Obviously, words alone are not enough, and we should let our actions speak too. Jesus taught us the principle of solidarity out of love, sharing what we have with our brothers and sisters *(see Basics)*. Jesus showed that it is up to us to change the world and the living conditions of people. If you ask why some have everything and others nothing, that is not God's fault, but ours! It is up to us to change this situation of injustice. So let's get started, inspired by Jesus and guided by the principles presented in this book.

It can be helpful to remind yourself sometimes that you too will die one day. Not out of a morbid fixation on death, but to help you consider: 'If today is going to be my last day, am I going to do something different?' If you are completely at peace with yourself and with God, the answer is 'no': you will live your last day just as you try to live every day, loving God and loving your neighbour.

The cross

You cannot personally change the situation of everyone. So how can you live happily while other people suffer? This is where Jesus' suffering on the cross takes a new dimension. He suffered and died for one reason only: to make it possible for you to be stronger than your negative tendencies and sins, and to live for love alone. Jesus made it possible for you to receive God's forgiveness for your sins, and live joyfully with him once more *(see #TwGOD 1.26-1.28)*.

But how can you be happy while others are suffering? First of all because God created you to be happy: "Rejoice in the Lord always; again I will say, Rejoice" *(Phil 4:4)*. The suffering of this life is not the end. Thanks to Jesus' sacrifice on the cross a better life is waiting in heaven for those who are suffering now *(see Explore)*. That is a good reason to be happy, even when not everything is perfect yet.

EXPLORE

The promise of happiness

Jesus gave us the eight beatitudes, which show that happiness is not only of this world, but always connected to our future in heaven. For that reason it is very Christian to be happy (blessed), even when we or others are suffering:

1. "Blessed are the poor in spirit, for theirs is the kingdom of heaven.
2. Blessed are those who mourn, for they will be comforted.
3. Blessed are the meek, for they will inherit the earth.
4. Blessed are those who hunger and thirst for righteousness, for they will be filled.
5. Blessed are the merciful, for they will receive mercy.
6. Blessed are the pure in heart, for they will see God.
7. Blessed are the peacemakers, for they will be called children of God.
8. Blessed are those who are persecuted for righteousness' sake, for theirs is the kingdom of heaven...

Rejoice and be glad, for your reward is great in heaven" *(Mt 5:1-12)*.

READ MORE

#TwGOD 1.26-1.28, 1.36-1.37, 4.1-4.2;
#OnlineSaints 1.39, 2.30.
Cross & Happiness: CCC 613-618 & 1716-1724;
CCCC 122-123 & 359-362;
YOUCAT 101-102 & 281-285; DOCAT 209 & 17.

PRAY

Dear Lord, you are especially close to all those who are suffering. Help me to support them where I can and see how our lives will be perfect only with you in heaven.

Faith and works: prayer

The Bible calls us to have faith and to pray for those in need *(1 Tim 2:1; see #TwGOD 3.1)*. Saint James added that faith without good deeds is dead: "If a brother or sister is naked and lacks daily food, and one of you says to them, 'Go in peace; keep warm and eat your fill', and yet you do not supply their bodily needs, what is the good of that?" *(Jas 2:15-16)*. You can do a lot to help others. But good deeds are not enough! Jesus invites us to believe in him, and rebukes us, just as he did with the Apostles when they did not really believe they could help someone in need *(Mt 17:14-20)*. Yes, we need to do what we can to help the poor and needy, but our work will always be insufficient. Still, however desperate the situation may seem, there is always hope. A hope founded on faith. Jesus came to announce the broadest perspective of life, which is our future with him in heaven. Until we are there, we need to do what we can to change the situation in the world with our hands, while bringing all the suffering in the world to God in our prayer.

QUOTE

Integral conversion

"We must... encourage and support the 'ecological conversion'... At stake is... also a 'human' ecology which makes the existence of creatures more dignified, by protecting the fundamental good of life in all its manifestations and by preparing for future generations an environment more in conformity with the creator's plan."

[Pope John Paul II, General audience, 17 Jan. 2001]

"We are in need of an ecological conversion... This conversion must be understood in an integral way, as a transformation of how we relate to our sisters and brothers, to other living beings, to creation in all its rich variety and to the Creator who is the origin and source of all life."

[Pope Francis, World Day of Peace, 1 Jan. 2020, 4]

SAINT

Joy to the world

Philip Neri dedicated his life to the poor and outcast of Rome. He knew what suffering was and must have been frustrated that he could not help everyone. Still, he was a very joyful man, who told many a joke and laughed a lot. Philip dedicated a lot of time to prayer. For example, together with some friends he would take turns to pray for 40 hours in the presence of Jesus in the Eucharist.

THINK

- How can you contribute to a fairer distribution of goods and opportunities?
- What will you answer when people say that God does not act?
- Can prayer change the situation of people in the world? Why (not)?
- Do you think you can be happier after reading this book? Why (not)?

ACT

Do I need to convert?

You may think of yourself as quite a good person. You share, you recycle, you participate, and you are tolerant. So why would you need to convert?

- We need a personal conversion in order to dedicate our life to Jesus and his teaching. But even then it is so easy to be led astray by selfish thoughts or actions. So you will need to convert every day again, returning to your original promise to God. Only with him at your side can you face the horrors of the world. Do you want to turn to God?
- We need a social conversion because there are structures of sin in our communities and societies *(see Question 12)*. Neither individuals nor societies can hide behind the excuse of what others do or not do. Conversion is about you. In what areas do you see the need for social conversion?
- We need an ecological conversion in which our relationship with Jesus leads to a new way of relating to the world around us *(see Quote)*. What would this mean for you?
- Every conversion means coming closer to Jesus. We can help others to approach the moment of conversion, but it really should be their personal choice. So all you can do is gently present and explain to them the beauty of the answers that we can find in God alone *(see Question 26)*. How would you do that?

Only through a personal and collective conversion can we make the world resemble the great place that God wants it to be, always realising that this is but a faint prelude of what is awaiting us in heaven!

RECAP

God intended the world to be different, but we made it into what it is. We need to convert to see what he intended. Jesus' love brings us happiness now and in heaven.

Can we solve hunger by evangelisation?

Why does God want me to give witness of my faith? Can I evangelise through my profession?

Jesus told his followers: "Go into all the world and proclaim the Gospel to the whole creation" *(Mk 16:15)*. It is a Christian duty to inform others of the beauty of our faith. While it is up to them to accept the faith, it is up to us to give them a chance to know the support and inspiration that a life with Jesus will bring them.

The first way to proclaim the faith is by living it. A Christian who speaks eloquently about Jesus but does not apply the basic principles of love in their personal life is a poor evangeliser. We need to live solidarity in all aspects of our lives. Prayer is a form of solidarity too. We share the lives of people by bringing them before God in our prayer. We intercede for them: we ask God to help them and invite the saints to pray with us *(see #TwGOD 4.15; #OnlineSaints 2.7)*.

More than bread

Solidarity with the poor means more than sharing our bread. As Jesus said: "One does not live by bread alone, but by every word that comes from the mouth of God" *(Mt 4:4)*. By sharing our bread, we put into practice what Jesus taught us to do *(Mt 14:16)*. And if we share our faith with those who are spiritually poor, we do so in order to satisfy the spiritual hunger of people, also in line with what Jesus taught us. The one cannot go without the other.

Obviously it is not enough to send a shipment of bibles in response to famine, although physical need is always accompanied by spiritual need. As long as there is hunger in the world, emergency aid in the form of food supplies is a great necessity to alleviate human suffering. And integral human development demands attention to the entire human being, including their spiritual wellbeing *(see Basics)*. Considered thus, the proclamation of the faith is a true work of mercy *(see About this book)*.

Heavenly social justice

If all people in the world always lived in accordance with Jesus' teachings, we would live in a soothing environment of justice and peace *(see Question 10)*. Our striving for justice and peace foreshadows the heavenly life we have been promised by Jesus. He has conquered what is evil in the world by opening the path to eternal life in peace with God *(Jn 16:33)*. The prophet Isaiah foresaw this peace when he prophesised: "The wolf shall live with the lamb... The nursing child shall play over the hole of the asp... They will not hurt or destroy" *(Isa 11:6-9)*. That is not only a vision of the future paradise in heaven: we can contribute to making this happen partly here and now if we strive for the integral development of every human being, serving both their physical and spiritual needs.

God needs you!

Do not despair, with the help of God you can do the impossible and help change the world, first of all by your lifestyle and your prayer. He needs you, although you may not see it that way. Take courage, you can make a difference! It is to you that Saint Paul wrote: "I thank my God every time I remember you, constantly praying with joy in every one of my prayers for all of you, because of your sharing in the gospel... I am confident of this, that [God] who began a good work among you will bring it to completion by the day of Jesus Christ" *(Phil 1:3-6)*.

READ MORE

#TwGOD 4.49-4.50; #OnlineSaints 1.16-1.20.
Evangelisation & Freedom: CCC 91, 849-856, 2044-2046 & 2104-2109; CCCC 172-173, 433, 444; YOUCAT 11, 133, 347 & 354; DOCAT 30.

EXPLORE

Online missionaries

Jesus calls everyone to be a missionary, going into all the world *(Mk 16:15)*. For ages, the Church has sent out missionaries to preach even in the most remote areas. But have you ever realised that there is a whole new 'continent' where we are called to bring the Gospel? Pope Benedict XVI called on especially the young to help evangelise the 'digital continent'. With so many people spending hours online, it is imperative that we help them discover the beauty of the Gospel for their lives. The pope wrote: "Human hearts are yearning for a world where love endures, where gifts are shared, where unity is built, where freedom finds meaning in truth, and where identity is found in respectful communion" *(24 Jun. 2009)*. Our faith in Jesus is a great gift to pass on, as it can respond to these expectations. You too can be an online missionary!

PRAY

Dear God, help me to care for the body and soul of my neighbour, while living my relationship with you in all honesty as a witness for the world.

Growing in holiness

The social teaching of the Church can help you grow in holiness in daily life. Through your daily choices you can more and more become one with Jesus. These daily choices include choosing fair and ecological products *(see Question 5)*, recycling and reducing waste *(see Question 6)*, giving to the poor and homeless *(see Question 1)*, spreading peace around you *(see Question 14)*, participating in society *(see Question 20)*... When you are sent out after Mass, e.g.: 'Go in peace, glorifying the Lord by your life', that is not the end of your worship, but the beginning of your renewed relationship with Jesus in the world! A relationship that calls you to share your faith and all you have with your brothers and sisters. Thus you will grow in holiness yourself and come closer to Jesus.

QUOTE

Instrument of evangelisation

"The Church's social teaching is itself a valid instrument of evangelisation. As such, it proclaims God and his mystery of salvation in Christ to every human being, and for that very reason reveals man to himself. In this light, and only in this light, does it concern itself with everything else: the human rights of the individual, and in particular of the 'working class', the family and education, the duties of the state, the ordering of national and international society, economic life, culture, war and peace, and respect for life from the moment of conception until death." **[Pope John Paul II, Centesimus Annus, 54]**

"Christian life requires dynamism, and it requires a willingness to walk, allowing the Holy Spirit to guide... The world needs Christians who allow themselves to be moved, who do not tire of walking on life's streets, to bring the comforting Word of Jesus to everyone. Every baptised person has received the vocation to proclaim... Jesus!" **[Pope Francis, Angelus, 2 Feb. 2020]**

SAINT

God's social network

Carlo Acutis had a passion for computers, and an even greater passion for God. He used his gadgets to tell people about God as one of the first online missionaries. He wanted to encourage people to be more themselves, just as they were created and loved by God. His closeness to Jesus helped him to calmly receive the news of his lethal disease. He was 15 years old when he died.

THINK

- Do you need to be perfect in order to witness and speak about your faith? Why (not)?
- Is a badly behaving Christian an anti-evangeliser? Why (not)?
- What is your personal motivation for speaking about the faith (or not)?
- Should we speak less of politics and economics and more of the salvation of souls? Why (not)?

ACT

How can I evangelise through my profession?

You are in a great position to reach people through the Gospel.

- 'Why would I want to evangelise?' For starters because Jesus tells you to do so *(Mk 16:15)*. Your faith gives you strength and joy, something you wish also for others. Priests and nuns are but a small percentage of all Christians: is it right to leave all evangelisation work to them? You can go where they cannot. Did you ever see yourself as a missionary?
- 'Isn't it through my deeds that I should proclaim the faith first?' Absolutely! You need to live in coherence with your faith, and thus give witness of your relationship with Jesus. However, often it is important to speak too. Not in the way a learned theologian would do, but in your own words, with examples of every day. Do you think you can do that?
- 'They won't listen to me', you may object. When Moses said the same, God got very angry *(Ex 4:10-17)*. He promises you the help of the Holy Spirit *(Lk 12:11-12)*. There is no need to worry about what you will say and how. Rather, be concerned about the other person, listen to them and their difficulties, and, when you deem the moment right, share in a humble way about your relationship with Jesus. What are you afraid of?
- 'What if they refuse to accept the faith?' You cannot change people's hearts: God created them free to choose for or against him. Be patient and let people feel that you leave them free too. Are you ready for such holy indifference?

You can contribute greatly to the proclamation of the Gospel in today's world if you live your life with Jesus in close communion with him and let yourself be led by the social teaching of the Church.

RECAP

The Gospel can satiate the great spiritual hunger of our world, while we need to share our bread too. Through the example of your life you give witness of God, also at work.

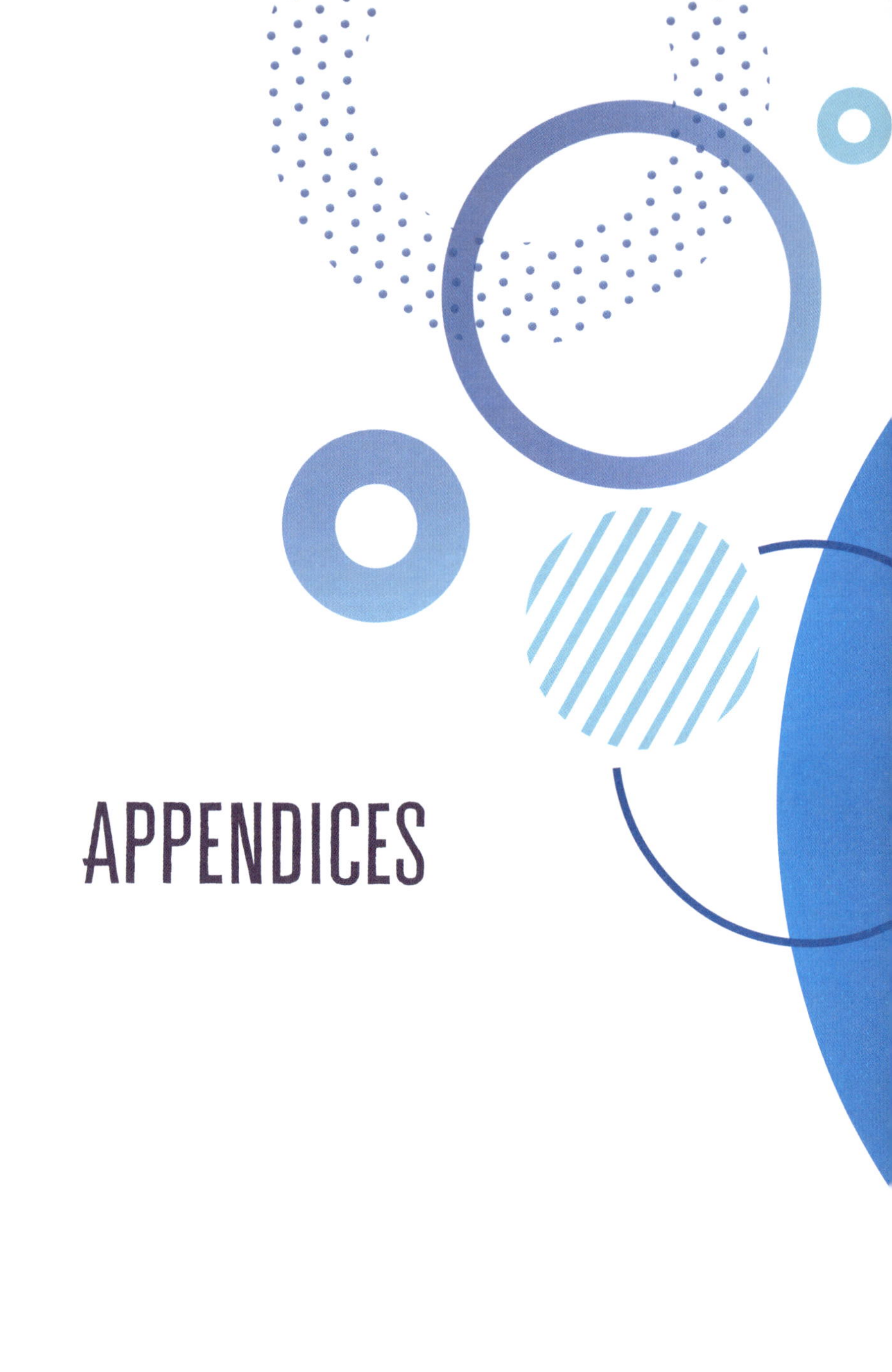

APPENDICES

APPENDIX 1: THE BOOKS OF THE BIBLE

OLD TESTAMENT

Gen	Genesis	Prov	Proverbs
Ex	Exodus	Eccl	Ecclesiastes
Lev	Leviticus	Song	Song of Solomon
Num	Numbers	Wis	Wisdom
Deut	Deuteronomy	Sir	Sirach (Ecclesiasticus)
Josh	Joshua	Isa	Isaiah
Judg	Judges	Jer	Jeremiah
Ruth	Ruth	Lam	Lamentations
1 Sam	1 Samuel	Bar	Baruch
2 Sam	2 Samuel	Ez	Ezekiel
1 Kgs	1 Kings	Dan	Daniel
2 Kgs	2 Kings	Hos	Hosea
1 Chr	1 Cronicles	Joel	Joel
2 Chr	2 Cronicles	Am	Amos
Ezra	Ezra	Ob	Obadiah
Neh	Nehemiah	Jon	Jonah
Tob	Tobit	Mic	Micah
Jdt.	Judith	Nah	Nahum
Esth	Esther	Hab.	Habakkuk
1 Mc	1 Maccabees	Zeph	Zephaniah
2 Mc	2 Maccabees	Hag.	Haggai
Job	Job	Zech	Zechariah
Ps	Psalms	Mal	Malachi

NEW TESTAMENT

Mt	Matthew	1 Tim	1 Timothy
Mk	Mark	2 Tim	2 Timothy
Lk	Luke	Ti	Titus
Jn	John	Phlm	Philemon
Acts	Acts of the Apostles	Heb	Hebrews
Rom	Romans	Jas	James
1 Cor	1 Corinthians	1 Pt	1 Peter
2 Cor	2 Corinthians	2 Pt	2 Peter
Gal	Galatians	1 Jn	1 John
Eph	Ephesians	2 Jn	2 John
Phil	Philippians	3 Jn	3 John
Col	Colossians	Jude	Jude
1 Thess	1 Thessalonians	Rev	Revelation (Apocalypse)
2 Thess	2 Thessalonians		

APPENDIX 2: FOUNDATIONAL DOCUMENTS OF THE SOCIAL TEACHING OF THE CHURCH

Pope Leo XIII, ***Rerum Novarum***, 1891

The dignity and rights of workers are to be upheld at all moments, also in the wake of the industrial revolution. They have a right to property and to assemble in worker's unions. Justice for all should be a reality, with special care for the poor and weak.

Pope Pius XI, ***Quadragesimo Anno***, 1931

Forty years after *Rerum Novarum*, the pope called for a more just division of power and wealth in answer to the economic depression, especially on the basis of the principles of solidarity and subsidiarity.

Pope John XXIII, ***Mater et Magistra***, 1961

The inhabitants of the earth should strive for the common good of the one community they form together. The social teaching of the Church is applied to developing countries and agriculture. The faithful play an important role in changing the world.

Pope John XXIII, ***Pacem in Terris***, 1963

Passionately the pope called for peace in a world which is split between nuclear powers. Peace is to be based on mutual trust, and flows forth from a just attention for the rights and duties of individuals, communities, and nations.

Second Vatican Council, ***Gaudium et Spes***, 1965

In a rapidly changing world, it is the role of the Church to come up with new responses which are based on the eternal truth of the Gospel. Human dignity, peace, the human good, and justice are essential principles for believers and all people of good will.

Pope Paul VI, ***Populorum Progressi***o, 1967

An integral human development is needed in response to structural poverty and the marginalisation of minorities. Profit and excessive property cannot be the only aim in life. A renewed attention for fundamental human rights is needed.

Pope Paul VI, ***Octogesima Adveniens***, 1971

Eighty years after *Rerum Novarum*, the pope recruited all faithful to formulate an answer to the situation in the world by participating in social life and thus work for its reform, also on the political level.

Pope Paul VI, ***Evangelii Nuntiandi***, 1975

Evangelisation, the spreading of the Gospel is a fundamental task of every Christian, not only of clergy and religious. As images have an ever greater importance, the image of our lives through which we give testimony of our faith should correspond with the Gospel.

Pope John Paul II, ***Laborem Exercens***, 1981

The dignity of work is essential in the support of human dignity. The rights of workers need to be upheld, and the unions should play an important role. People take precedence over property, and work is more important than capital.

Pope John Paul II, ***Solicitudo Rei Socialis***, 1987

There is a great need to convert structures of sin into true solidarity with the poor. This conversion can be stimulated by preaching the Gospel and giving testimony of Christian life. True development should involve all the world, and consider the entire human person.

Pope John Paul II, ***Centesimus Annus***, 1991

One hundred years after *Rerum Novarum*, the pope warned that we need to have the right view on who and what the human being is in itself. Its intrinsic dignity, human rights, justice and peace, are all essential in our striving for the common good.

Pope John Paul II, ***Evangelium Vitae***, 1995

God is the source of all life. He has a special love for the poor and marginalised. In response to the 'culture of death', the pope recalled that human life is something infinitely holy, and needs to be protected from its conception until natural death.

Pope Benedict XVI, ***Deus Caritas Est***, 2005

The pope distinguished possessive love (*eros*), self-giving love (*agape*) and love between friends (*philia*). God's commandment to love becomes concrete in the social charity activities of the Church, and should be based on a personal relationship with Christ.

Pope Benedict XVI, ***Caritas in Veritate***, 2009

The social teaching of the Church should flow forth from love and strive for justice for all in search for the common good. Justice and love are closely related, and shed a new light on business ethics and the economic crisis.

Pope Francis, ***Evangelii Gaudium***, 2013

The joy of the Gospel must be shared with the world by our communities, which are missionary by nature. This goes hand in hand with caring for the poor and needy, adapting structures of injustice and inequality, and every form of Christian love.

Pope Francis, ***Laudato si'***, 2015

The earth is our common home and God's creation, which needs to be protected and the fruits of which need to be shared. The Gospel is the answer to the current crisis. A global conversion is needed to promote an integral human development for all.

Pope Francis, ***Fratelli Tutti***, 2020

Fraternity and social friendship are the way towards a better world marked by justice and peace. Making an effective stance against war, violence, and indifference can only be achieved by the fraternal involvement of all people and institutions.

INDEX OF SAINTS

INDEX OF SUBJECTS

SHARE YOUR QUESTIONS, DISCOVER THE LOGIC OF FAITH, AND SEE HOW EVERYTHING IS CONNECTED!

What if communicating with God were as simple as posting or liking on social media? Whether your favourite tool is Instagram, Facebook, or Twitter, the multimedia initiative *Tweeting with GOD* helps you to see how simple it is to relate to God, even when you are offline!

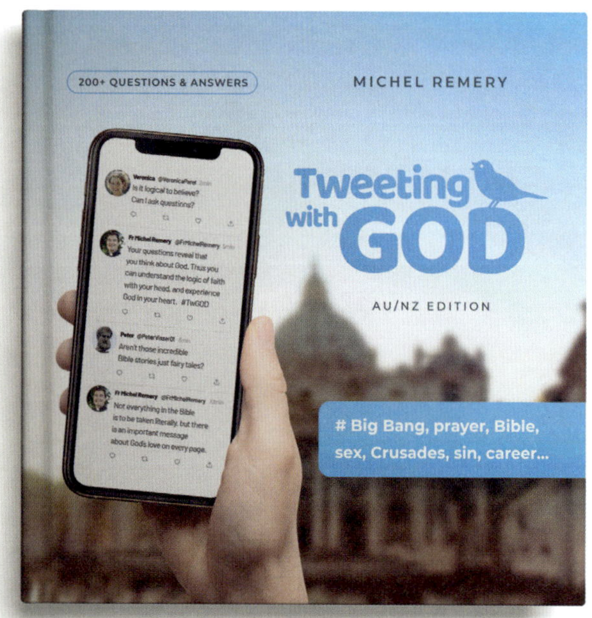

THE BOOK

- 200+ questions of young people answered, searching for the reasons why
- Fun facts, prayers, and thought-provoking quotes
- M. Remery, ***Tweeting with GOD***. *Big Bang, prayer, Bible, sex, Crusades, sin, career...*, Freedom Publishing Books 2017

MODERN TECHNOLOGY

Through a close integration between social media, modern technology and printed books, *Tweeting with GOD* (#TwGOD) wants to help you discover answers to your questions about the faith. The project was brought to life by young people with many questions, who keep searching for the meaning of their relationship with Jesus in their lives. Alone or in a group, you can find answers to your questions through *Tweeting with GOD.*

DOWNLOAD THE FREE APP
TWEETING WITH GOD

Use this interactive tool to discover more about the faith on the go:

- Follow Mass or concelebrate in 20+ languages
- Pray the Rosary and many other Catholic prayers in 20+ languages
- Find a brief answer to 200+ burning questions
- Scan the book *Tweeting with GOD* to find online extras

www.tweetingwithgod.com

A LIFE-CHANGING COURSE TO EXPLORE THE FAITH, SEARCH FOR ANSWERS OR PREPARE FOR THE SACRAMENTS

What if growing in faith were just as easy, natural, and contemporary as interacting on social media? The course ***How to grow in faith*** shows that it is just that! You will find an opportunity to ask questions, search for answers in groups, and discover how God loves each of us very deeply!

MULTIMEDIA RESOURCES

Online resources, videos, mobile apps, social media, and manifold activities make this a very interactive course. Every meeting begins with a question which helps the participants to explore their personal faith, through interactive exercises and profound dialogue. This results in a very interactive program that challenges the participants to truly participate while searching together for answers that will reveal the truth about life, love and faith.

www.howtogrowinfaith.com

PERSONALISED PROGRAM

The proposed course consists of 18 meetings on the sacraments and Christian life. If you need more than the proposed meetings, you can add some related questions from the ***Tweeting with GOD*** book and find more suggestions for themes in the appendix. The program can be spread over one, two, three and even more years, with extra material available. Free downloads make the course complete!

A COURSE FOR PEOPLE OF ALL GENERATIONS

The course can be used by schools as a program for religious education, by communities as a catechetical program to grow in faith, or by parishes to support those preparing for the Sacraments of Confirmation or First Holy Communion, catechumens seeking Baptism (RCIA), or couples preparing for Marriage. Think also of the personal development of teachers, health and social workers...

"This course is intended as a joint adventure for people who are searching, questioning, doubting... and above all desiring to grow."

Father Michel Remery - Author

POWERED BY

@OnlineWithSaints

/OnlineSaints

Online with Saints

DISCOVER FRIENDS AND COMPANIONS ON YOUR PATH TO GOD

Imagine you could meet and greet a saint, which saint would you choose? The multimedia content of the *Online with Saints* book offers a virtual encounter with 100+ saints from all around the world. Women and men, carpenters and scholars, mothers and popes, princes and paupers: their inspiring life stories are linked to real life modern questions, and together with them answers are found.

YOUR PATH TO SAINTHOOD

Anyone can become a saint! Every saint is different, with their own unique personality and destiny. Each of them found their vocation in a different way – demonstrating that God has a special plan and individual vocation for each individual. Online with Saints invites you to discern your own personal journey towards sanctity.

GET THE BOOK:

M. Remery, Online with Saints.
Discover friends and companions on your path to God, Freedom Publishers 2018.

LEARN MORE AND DOWNLOAD THE APP

APP

Let the saints tell their story in the first person by video. The *Online with Saints* app contains saints profiles, with interesting facts, quotes, prayers, and captivating stories of personal faith, love, and sacrifice. You can even take a selfie with the saint of choice. Obviously, it is possible to share discoveries on social media. Also, you can personalise the app through your *Online with Saints* profile.

DOWNLOAD THE FREE APP

Discover much more information about the saints:

- Social media profiles of the saints
- Animated videos about their lives
- Information on their history
- Pray with the saints & find patron saints

ONTWIKKELD DOOR

Tweeting with GOD

www.onlinewithsaints.com

NOTES

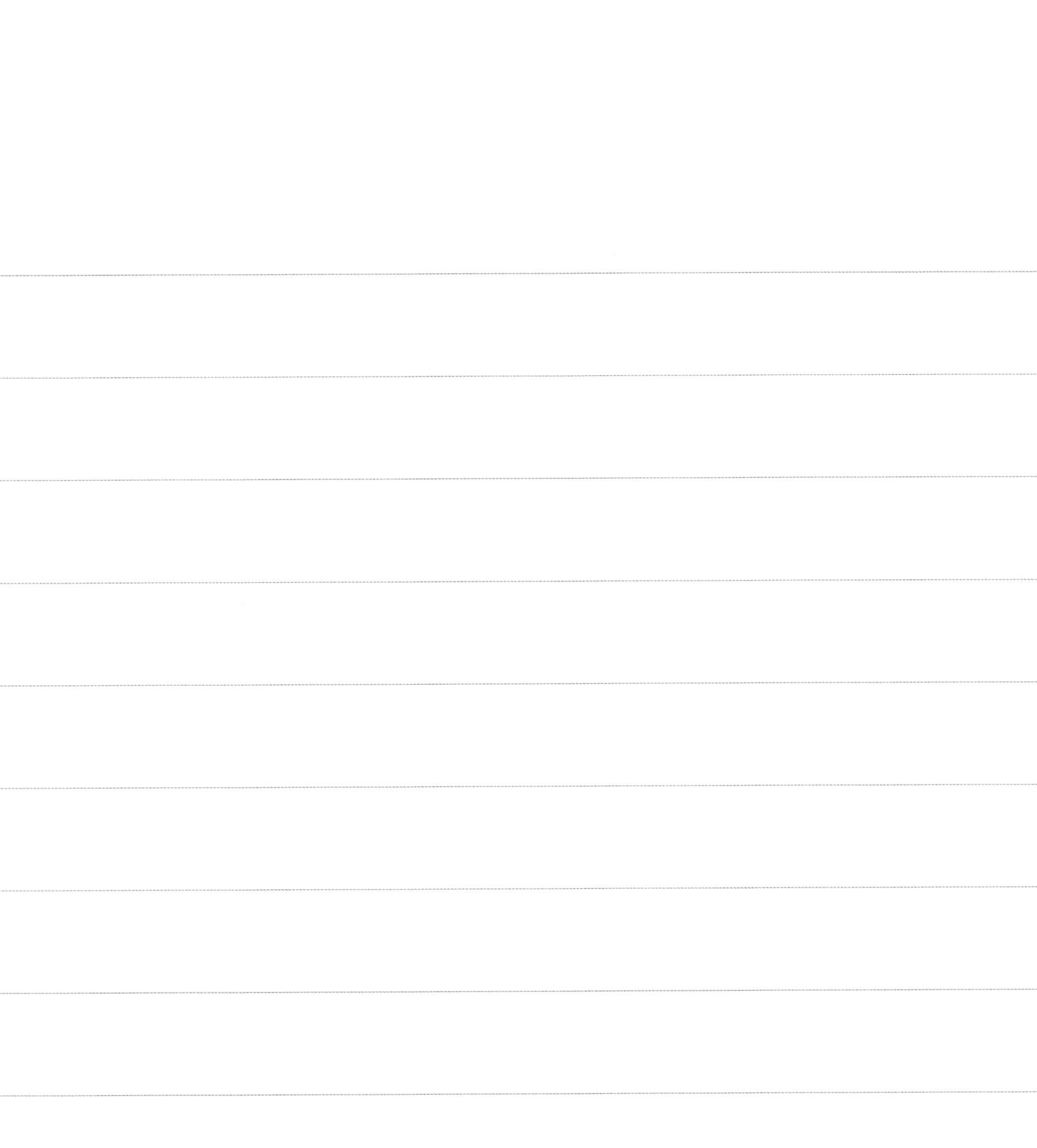

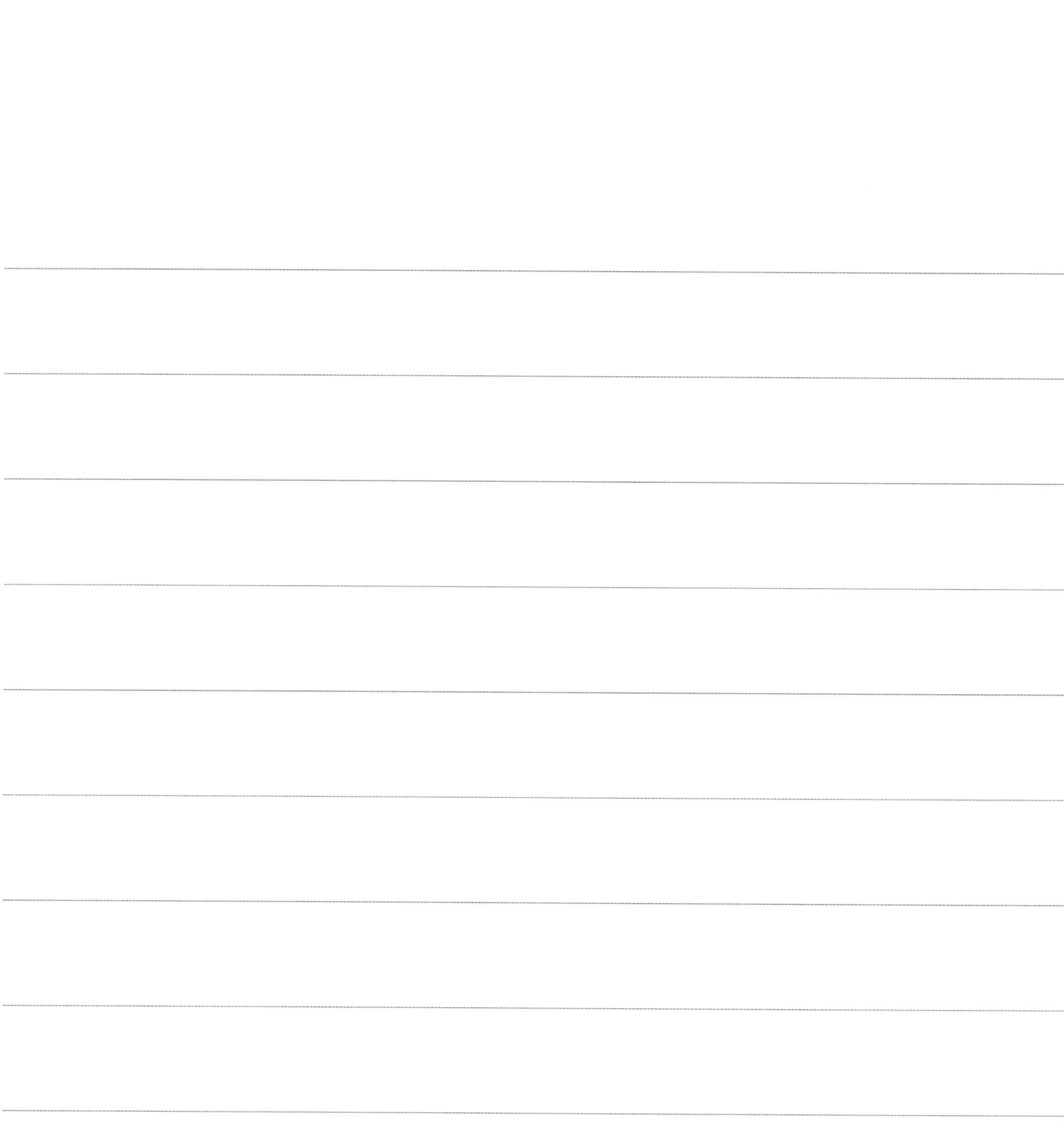

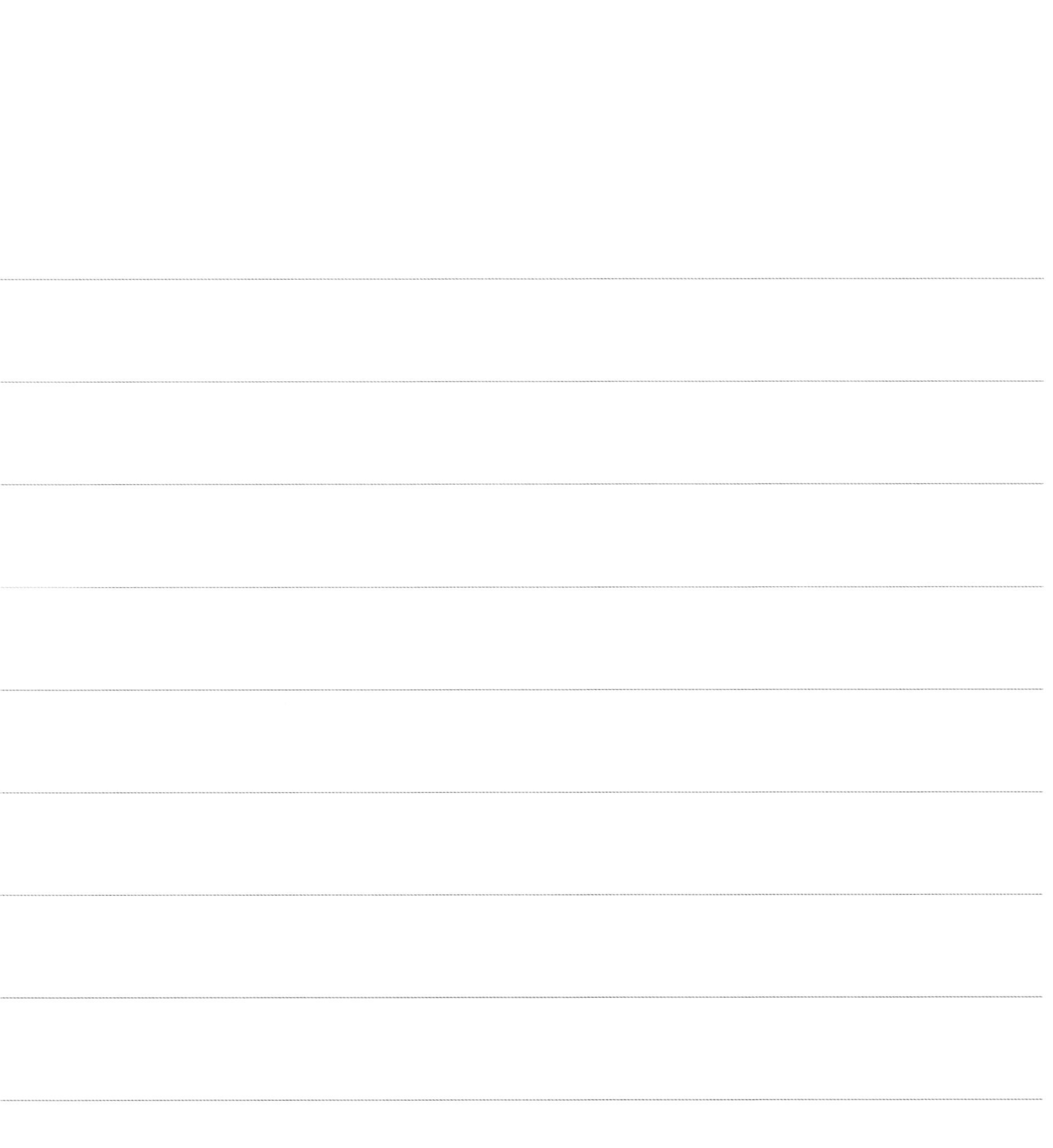

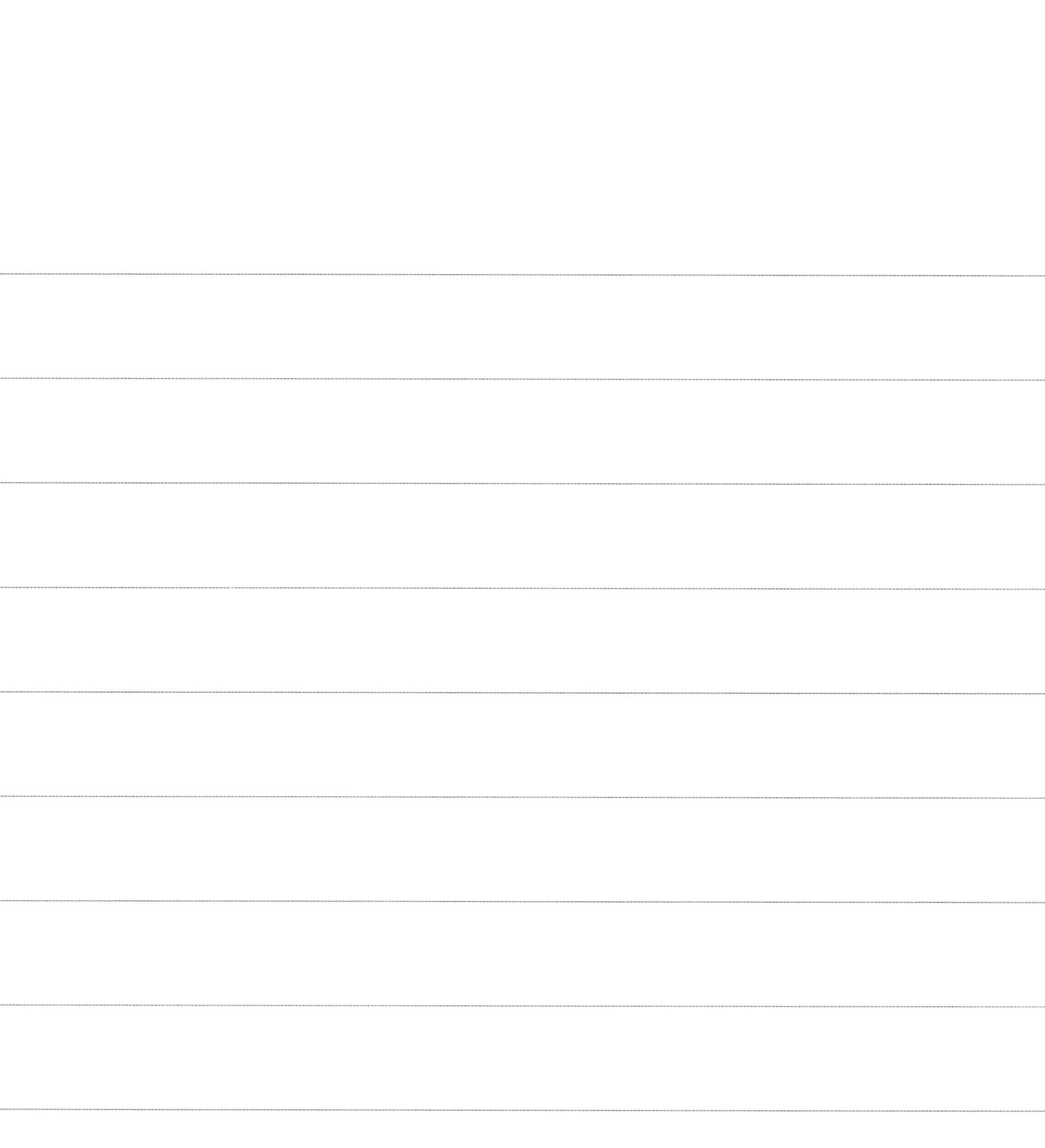

THANK YOU...

To His Eminence J.C. Cardinal Hollerich S.J., Archbishop of Luxembourg,
for insisting that this book should be written.

To Professor Dr P.J.J. van Geest, member of the Pontifical Theological Academy,
and Prof. Dr A.H.M. van Iersel, professor for moral theology and chaplaincy studies,
for reading the manuscript.

Also to L. Amaro (USA), A. & A.A. Andrew (Malaysia),
Vice Admiral M.J.M. Borsboom (Netherlands), J. Bullat (Sweden), J. Carneiro (Brazil),
B. Carpenter (USA), R. van Dijk (Netherlands), N. Douglas (Australia), A. Farthing (Australia),
J. van Halem (Netherlands), L. & V. Košak (Croatia), M. Król (Poland), S. Leka (Albania),
D. Loos (Belgium), C. Meijers (Luxembourg), L. Miranda (Brazil), I. Potworowski (Canada),
N. Pucheu (Dominican Republic), A.L. Reyes Rodríguez (Honduras),
L. Ribeiro de Mendonça (Brazil), Fr J.H. Smith (Netherlands), O.M. San Lucas Ceballos (Ecuador),
B. Schoo (Netherlands), A. Smolnik (Poland), M. Svobodová (Czech Republic),
A. Szargiej (Germany), R. Tolmik (Estonia), Fr R. Vincent (India), L. Zevallos (USA).

www.tweetingwithgod.com

   /TweetingwithGOD  @TwGOD_en

www.onlinewithsaints.com

  /OnlinewithSaints  Online With Saints

YOUR NEIGHBOUR IS GOD

26 SOCIAL QUESTIONS FOR A BETTER WORLD

www.yourneighbourisgod.com